Sous Vide:
Help for the Busy Cook

Harness the Power of Sous Vide to
Create Great Meals
Around Your Busy Schedule

By Jason Logsdon

Part of the *Cooking Sous Vide* Series

Presented By CookingSousVide.com

ISBN-13: 978-1466381285

ISBN-10: 1466381280

TABLE OF CONTENTS

Sous Vide Around Your Schedule

We have a fan page on Facebook. You can follow us there for updated recipes, tips, and equipment reviews.

You can find it at:
http://on.fb.me/jILtp0

In this day and age it is always a balancing act for busy families to try and get great tasty meals on the table. Sous vide has many characteristics that make it ideally suited to working around busy schedules.

BENEFITS FOR BUSY FAMILIES

Sous vide has many benefits for people who are busy or working during the day. These benefits can be used to get great meals on the table with a minimal amount of effort while working around your schedule.

Margin of Doneness

The first benefit is the wide margin of doneness that food cooked sous vide has. Most meats have a wide time frame, usually several hours, where they remain perfectly cooked. This is crucial when dealing with schedules that change due to working late or errands taking longer than expected. You can read more in the Doneness Range section of the Time and Temperature Charts chapter.

Hands Off Cooking

Another benefit is that the actual cooking of the food requires no attention and can be done when no one is home. This is similar to a crock pot, where you can put the food on and not worry about it until you get home.

Long Cooking Times

Sous vide has a reputation for long cooking times and needing advanced planning. However, this isn't always bad since many of us already have to plan meals ahead of time and we know when we'd like to eat due to work and family schedules. In addition, the long times used in sous vide can be perfect for making sure your food is done at the end of the day when you want

dinner to be ready.

Separation of Stages

One of the biggest benefits to using sous vide is the ability to separate the different cooking stages. This allows you to put in the hands-on time at one point, do the actual cooking at a different time, and finish the dish at a third point. We flesh out this benefit more in the following section.

STAGES OF SOUS VIDE

Like many cooking methods sous vide usually has three distinct stages. These are the prep stage or *Pre-Bath* in sous vide, the *Cooking* stage when the food is actually being cooked in the water bath, and the *Finishing* stage when everything comes together. Only the *Pre-Bath* and *Finishing* stages are active with sous vide since the actual cooking doesn't require any attention.

Understanding these stages and how they interact is vital to getting the most convenience out of sous vide cooking.

Pre-Bath Stage

The *Pre-Bath* stage is the first stage of sous vide cooking. It is everything you do to the food before bagging it. Breaking down larger cuts of meat, seasoning the food, and splitting it into portions is all done here. For the recipes in this book we've tried to keep this stage as quick as possible.

Cooking Stage

The *Cooking* stage consists of the time the food is in the water bath. With sous vide there is no hands-on work so the food can be cooked while you are away. Depending on the type of food the length of this stage can vary widely. We can plan meals around our busy schedules by using these variable cooking times.

There are many foods that take from 8 to 12 hours to cook and these are great for cooking during the day while you are working or away from the house. There are also many meats that take multiple days and these work well since they can be put in the bath later in an evening and will be ready a fews days later. Finally, there are also many things that can be cooked in under 2 hours, especially fish which can be done in 15 to 30 minutes.

Choosing foods with appropriate cooking times is critical to meal planning and a very easy way to get food on the table when you want it.

Finishing Stage

The *Finishing* stage is the final stage and entails everything done to the food once it is removed from the sous vide pouches. The addition of final seasonings and sauces, the searing process, creation of garnishes and sides all fall into this category. In this book we try to reduce the time of the finishing stage as much as possible to allow faster meal completion on the nights you want to eat.

SEPARATING THE STAGES

During most traditional cooking, especially by the home cook, each stage directly follows one another. You prep the food, cook it, and then finish it off. Sometimes you might prep a few ingredients an hour or two ahead of time but in general all three stages are done one after another.

Sous vide allows you to easily break this mold.

Because of the use of pouches in sous vide you can easily separate the stages to meet your schedule. The easiest way to spread out the stages is by using the refrigerator or freezer to hold the food between stages.

Between Stages: Pre-Bath to Cooking

As we saw in the *Cooking* stage, many sous vide meals can be put in the water bath in the morning before leaving the house or right as you get home. However, no one wants to be prepping food early in the morning. This is where sous vide comes in to separate the two stages.

With sous vide, you can easily separate the *Pre-Bath* stage from the *Cooking* stage by refrigerating or freezing the prepped and bagged food. The prepared pouch can then be placed directly into the water bath when you are ready to cook it without any additional work. Manipulating the amount of time between these stages is key to creating easy meals during the week with little to no work prepping the food.

Oftentimes we will prep our food the night before, after we've had dinner. That way it's ready the next day to put into the water bath. We will also prepare several meals at once and freeze them until needed. On the day we want to use them we just grab them from the freezer and place them directly into the water bath. Freezing can sometimes lead to slightly lower quality meals but it is hardly noticeable.

Between Stages: Cooking to Finishing

The above method works great for foods whose cooking times fit around a typical work day but sometimes that doesn't match up with your schedule. When that is the case you need to separate the *Cooking* and *Finishing* stages using the cook, chill, and hold method.

We will go into more details later but the basic concept behind cook, chill, and hold is after cooking the food sous vide you chill it and then can refrigerate or freeze it until needed. This allows you to complete the *Cooking* stage on the weekend or later some evening during the week, chill the food, and then wait days or even months before moving into the *Finishing* stage. It also allows you to save time by preparing large batches of food at the same time and freezing them until you need them.

By keeping the time spent on the active stages shorter and correctly separating the stages you can easily make great meals planned around your schedule.

TYPES OF RECIPES

In this book we focus on four different types of recipes that use the variation in cooking times and the spacing between stages in different ways. Remember that the recipe types aren't exclusive and several foods can be done with multiple ones but we want to highlight the different methods and how they can be used to help you plan your meals.

Here is a short description of each one of our recipe types. Under each chapter you will also get a full description of the method and its nuances.

Day Of Meats

These recipes encompass meats that are cooked during a typical working day. The *Pre-Bath* stage can be done in the morning or on a previous day. The food is then added to the water bath in the morning and will be done 8 to 12 hours later. Some examples are flank steaks, sirloin roasts, and baby back ribs.

Some foods can also be cooked in this time frame such as pork chops and chicken breasts. They turn out drier than when cooked for lower times but they are still pretty good and a great time saver during the week.

Multi-Day Meats

Multi-Day Meats are things that take longer than twelve hours to cook. They will be put in the water bath up to several days before you want to eat. The key to them is to put them in the water bath at the right time so they will be done when you are ready to eat. The *Finishing* stage is then quickly completed the evening you are eating. Some examples are beef roasts, lamb shanks, and short ribs.

Fast Cookers

Fast Cookers are foods that have shorter cooking times by sous vide standards. They are foods that can be cooked once you get home as you prepare the rest of the meal. Some examples are fish, chicken breasts, and tender beef.

Cook, Chill, and Hold

Cook, chill, and hold is a widely used concept in the restaurant industry and it's very easy to apply the same concepts at home. You cook the food sous vide then chill the pouch in a bowl filled with ½ ice and ½ water until it is completely cold. At that point you can put it in the refrigerator for several days or freeze it for several months. When you are ready to eat, you warm it up, either in a water bath or by searing it, and then finish making the meal.

It is a great method for people who work or who have trouble finding 2 to 5 hours of cooking time before dinner. Several days before you want to eat you cook the food sous vide, chill it, and then refrigerate it until the night you want to eat. You can also freeze it for several months with just a minor decrease in quality.

Bring the food up to temperature, usually a 20 to 40 minute process, finish the rest of the meal, and you are all set to eat. Any meat can be cooked with this method but in this book we focus mainly on foods that are cooked between 2 and 5 hours since they are hard to cook with sous vide if you are not home several hours before you want to eat.

Quick Sides

Our quick sides do not use sous vide but we wanted to include them as fast and tasty recipes you can add to many of the dishes in this book. They focus on using fresh vegetables to create a variety of dishes that can be done in 15 to 60 minutes.

SOUS VIDE BASICS

For a more detailed look at sous vide, the equipment needed,
and the specifics of the process you can view our free
Beginning Sous Vide guide on our website.

You can find them on our website at:
www.cookingsousvide.com/beginning-sous-vide-guide.html

HISTORY OF SOUS VIDE

Sous vide, or low temperature cooking, is the process of cooking food at a very tightly controlled temperature, normally the temperature the food will be served at. This is a departure from traditional cooking methods that use high heat to cook the food, which must be removed at the exact moment it reaches the desired temperature.

Sous vide was first used as an upscale culinary technique in kitchens in France in the 1970s and traditionally is the process of cooking vacuum sealed food in a low temperature water bath. This process helps to achieve texture and doneness not found in other cooking techniques, as well as introducing many conveniences for a professional kitchen. Sous vide has slowly been spreading around the world in professional kitchens everywhere and is finally making the jump to home kitchens.

As sous vide has become more popular and moved to the home kitchen the term now encompasses both traditional "under vacuum" sous vide and also low temperature cooking. Some preparations rely on the vacuum pressure to change the texture of the food but in most cases the benefits of sous vide are realized in the controlled, low temperature cooking process. This means that fancy vacuum sealers can be set aside for home sealers or even ziploc bags.

HOW IT WORKS

The basic concept of sous vide cooking is that food should be cooked at the temperature it will be served at. For instance, if you are cooking a steak to medium rare, you want to serve it at 131°F.

With traditional cooking methods you would normally cook it on a hot grill or oven at around 400°F-500°F and pull it off at the right moment when the middle has reached 131°F. This results in a bulls eye effect of burnt meat on the outside turning to medium rare in the middle. This steak cooked sous vide would be cooked at 131°F for several hours. This will result in the entire piece of meat being a perfectly cooked medium rare. The steak would then usually be quickly seared at high heat to add the flavorful, browned crust to it.

There are two basic components to sous vide cooking at home: temperature and time. Each one of these can affect the end quality, texture, and taste of sous vide dishes. Learning to understand how they affect the food is one of the most important things as you begin sous vide cooking.

Temperature

All sous vide cooking is done at temperatures below the boiling point of water and normally not above 185°F. You usually cook the food at the temperature you want it served at, so most settings are between 120°F and 185°F, depending on the food being prepared.

While the range of temperature used in sous vide is much less variable than for traditional cooking, the precise control of the temperature is of great importance. When you set your oven at 400°F it actually fluctuates about 50 degrees, sending it between 375°F and 425°F, which is fine when cooking at high temperatures. When cooking sous vide, the temperature of the water determines the doneness of your food, so a 50°F fluctuation would result in over-cooked food. Most sous vide machines fluctuate less than 1°F and the best are less than 0.1°F.

This precision is why many sous vide machines are very expensive. However, there are many more home machines available in the last few years, some good do-it-yourself kits, and even some ways to accomplish "accurate enough" sous vide on the cheap. We discuss many of your options in our free online Beginning Sous Vide Guide (http://bit.ly/e8MvOu).

Time

Cooking tenderizes food by breaking down its internal structure. This process happens faster at higher temperatures. Because sous vide is done at such low temperatures the cooking time needs to be increased to achieve the same tenderization as traditional techniques.

Also, your window of time to perfectly cooked food is much longer than with traditional cooking methods because you are cooking the food at the temperature you want it to end up at, rather than a higher temperature. This also allows you to leave food in the water bath even after it is done since keeping it at this temperature does not dry out the food, up to several hours longer for tougher cuts of meat. However, be careful not to take this concept too far as food can still become overcooked by sous vide, many times without showing it externally.

Temperature and Time Together

The power of sous vide cooking comes from precisely controlling both temperature and time. This is important because of the way meat reacts to different temperatures.

At 120°F meat slowly begins to tenderize as the protein myosin begins to coagulate and the connective tissue in the meat begins to break down. As the temperature increases so does the speed of tenderization.

However, meat also begins to lose its moisture above 140°F as the heat causes the collagen in the cells to shrink and wring out the moisture. This happens very quickly over 150°F and meat becomes completely dried out above 160°F.

Many tough cuts of meat are braised or roasted for a long period of time so the meat can fully tenderize, but because of the high temperatures they can easily become dried out. Using sous vide allows you to hold the meat below the 140°F barrier long enough for the slower tenderization process to be effective. This results in very tender meat that is still moist and not overcooked.

BASIC SOUS VIDE TECHNIQUE

At the heart of sous vide cooking is a very simple process. While there are variations within each dish, almost every sous vide meal follows the same steps.

Flavor the Food

Just like many traditional methods, you often times flavor the food before cooking it. This can be as simple as a sprinkling of salt and pepper or as complicated as adding an elaborate sauce, spice rub, or even smoking the food. Depending on the type of seasoning it can either be rubbed directly onto the food itself or added into the pouch with the food.

If you are using a normal home vacuum sealer and want to add more than a little liquid, freeze the liquid before adding it to the pouch. This way the process of vacuum sealing will not suck out the liquid. Otherwise, you can normally use food grade ziploc bags to seal food with liquids.

In our various food sections we give some tips and suggested recipes for flavoring your food. But remember, just like traditional cooking a lot of the fun comes with experimenting.

Seal the Food

Once the seasoning and food have been added to the pouch, remove the air and seal it closed. Removing the air results in closer contact between the food and the water in the water bath. This helps to facilitate quicker cooking since water transfers heat more efficiently than air.

Sealing the food can be done with anything from ziplocs or food grade plastic wrap to a FoodSaver Vacuum Sealer or even a chambered vacuum sealer. We discuss many of your options in our free online Beginning Sous Vide Guide (http://bit.ly/e8MvOu)

Some vacuum sealers have different strengths of vacuum to seal the bag and can be used to affect the texture of some types of food.

If you are using ziploc bags to seal your food you can use this trick to force out the majority of the air. Once the bag is ready to close, seal the bag except for 1" of it. Place the bag into the water bath making sure to keep that last 1" out of the water. The water will force the remaining air out of the bag and then you can seal it completely. When done properly this is almost as good as using a weak vacuum sealer and will work great for most low-temperature sous vide cooking.

Heat the Water

Simply bring the water bath up to the temperature you will cook at. This water bath will normally be the same temperature that you will want your food to end up at.

Depending on the type of heat regulator, you may be able to have the food in the water while it heats. For others, it is best to preheat the water before placing the food in it due to early fluctuations in temperature.

You can use anything from a pot on a stove to a beer cooler to a professional immersion circulator. We discuss many of your options in our free online Beginning Sous Vide Guide (http://bit.ly/e8MvOu)

Cook the Food

Put the food pouch in the water and let it cook for the amount of time specified in the recipe or on the Time and Temperature chart. For items that are cooked for longer amounts of time it can be good to rotate the food every 6 to 10 hours, especially if you are using less precise sous vide equipment.

At some higher temperatures the sous vide pouches can float due to air released from the food. If that happens you might have to use a plate or bowl to weight them down.

If you are unfamiliar with how sous vide cooking times work please read our Doneness Range section in the Time and Temperature Chart chapter.

Finish the Dish

To get a good finish and texture to your food, especially meats, it is usually advisable to quickly sear the meat. This is usually done in hot pan, on a grill, or with a culinary blow torch. Some meals also call for other methods of finishing the food, such as breading and deep-frying for chicken.

You can also quickly chill the food in an ice bath which is ½ ice and ½ water and then refrigerate or freeze the food for later re-heating.

SOUS VIDE SAFETY

Sous vide is a new and largely untested method of cooking. It potentially carries many inherent health risks that may not be fully understood. We have done our best to provide the latest information and what is currently understood about this form of cooking.

However, we feel that anyone undertaking sous vide cooking, or any other method of cooking, should fully inform themselves about any and all risks associated with it and come to their own conclusions about its safety. Following anything in this book may make you or your guests sick and should only be done if you are fully aware of the potential risks and complications.

There are two main concerns when it comes to sous vide cooking, they are pathogens and the dangers of cooking in plastic.

Pathogens, Bacteria and Salmonella

One large safety concern with sous vide that has been studied in great detail deals with the propagation of bacteria at various temperatures, especially salmonella. Salmonella only thrive in a certain range of temperatures, from about 40°F to 130°F (4°C to 54°C), often referred to as the "danger zone".

This danger zone is why we refrigerate our foods until an hour or so before we are ready to cook them. It is also why we cook our foods to specific temperatures before we eat them.

The biggest misconception about bacteria and the danger zone is that any food in the temperature range is not safe and as soon as you move above 130°F the food instantly becomes safe. The truth is that the bacteria begin to die in direct relation to the temperature they are exposed to.

The best way to visualize this is to think about how we humans react to heat. We do fine in climates where the temperature is below 100°F. However, once it begins to climb around 110°F or 120°F you begin to hear about deaths in the news due to heat stroke. If the temperature were to raise to 200°F stepping outside for more than a few seconds would kill you.

Bacteria behave in the exact same way. They begin to die at around 130°F to 135°F and 165°F just about instantly kills them. You can see this in the chart below, based on the USDA data replicated in the Required Cooking Time section. At 136°F it takes about 63 minutes for your food to be safe and at 146°F it only takes 7 minutes to become safe.

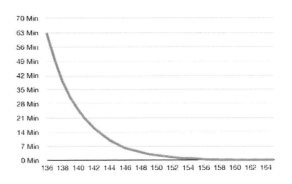

This concept is why the USDA recommends that chicken is cooked to 165°F, because at that temperature it takes only a few seconds for enough bacteria to die to achieve acceptable safety levels. In comparison, at 136°F it takes 63.3 minutes at that temperature to achieve the same safety level, something that is virtually impossible using traditional cooking methods. Using sous vide makes it possible to heat chicken and other meats to an internal temperature of as low as 130°F and hold it there long enough to kill the bacteria.

Please remember that this is assuming that your thermometer is exact and the water temperature is completely steady. I recommend always cooking foods at a little higher than the minimum temperature and a little longer than the minimum cooking time in order to account for any variance in temperature your equipment causes.

For more information about how long chicken, poultry, and beef need to be held at certain temperatures please refer to the USDA Guide mentioned in our Resources chapter. For more explanations of how this works you can reference the excellent guides by Douglas Baldwin or Serious Eats mentioned in our Resources chapter.

Plastic Safety

Another main concern of sous vide is cooking in plastic and whether or not this is a dangerous practice. Many scientists and chefs believe that cooking in food grade plastic at these low temperatures does not pose any risk, the temperature is about equivalent to leaving a bottle of water in your car, or in a semi during transport, in summer.

However, I find it hard to believe that we know everything about how plastic reacts to heat, water, our bodies, and the environment. As such, I encourage you to read up on the safety of plastic in sous vide and plastic in general and come to your own conclusions about the safety of using these techniques or consuming products packaged or shipped in plastic.

CONVERTING EXISTING RECIPES

If you have any questions you can ask them in the Sous Vide Forums on our website. Just post your question and other sous vide cooks will weigh in with their answers.

You can find them on our website at:
www.cookingsousvide.com/sous-vide-forums

Even though we provide more than a hundred recipes in this book we know we can't cover it all. One of the great things about sous vide is that it is easy to convert existing recipes into sous vide recipes with just a few tweaks. This means you can quickly convert the recipes from your favorite cookbooks into sous vide meals. There are three main steps to accomplish this.

DETERMINE THE METHOD TO USE

First look at the type of meat in the recipe and look up the time and temperature needed to cook it in the Time and Temperature Charts section. Now that you know how long it will cook for you can determine the recipe method to use. For instance, if it cooks for over 12 hours you will want to follow the Multi-Day Meats section. You can get a feel for the types of meats cooked using each method by scanning the recipes in each chapter.

Once you know the recipe method you will use you can follow the General Process guidelines in that section.

ISOLATE SEASONINGS

The next step in converting the recipe is to isolate the seasonings. Many foods are seasoned ahead of time with a rub or glaze and then cooked. While others have a sauce or crust added during or after the cooking process.

First look at the recipes and see what these seasonings are. Once you find the seasonings you need to determine whether they should be added before or after the sous vide process.

Season Before

Many recipes will call for spice rubs, marinades, or other similar seasonings. Throughout the marinating and cooking processes these flavors will melt into the meat and flavor it, and at the end of the cooking period they won't be distinct flavors.

These seasonings are the type you want to add before the sous vide process. You can add the spice rubs to the meat before bagging it or place fresh herbs like rosemary and thyme directly into the bags. In general it's best to substitute powdered garlic, onion, and ginger for their fresh counterparts, otherwise they can impart an off flavor.

Season After

Often times a recipe, especially steaks and chops, will have some sort of crust on it. While these crusts flavor the meat they don't break down during the cooking process like many rubs or marinades do. This means when you eat the meat you still get the distinct flavor and texture of the crust.

These are the types of seasonings to add after the meat is cooked sous vide. If you add a crust beforehand the moist sous vide process will quickly dissolve it. To get around this, once you take the meat out of the sous vide pouches you can dry it and then add the crust. Once you sear it the crust will be very similar to a traditional one.

Choose Your Finishing Method

One of the key things in most sous vide dishes is the finishing method used. The different methods add their flavors and textures to the meat. Depending on what the dish is and what you are trying to accomplish you will want to choose one of the following methods.

Pan Frying

Pan frying or pan searing is the most common method of finishing sous vide meats. It can usually be used instead of grilling with only a slight loss of the grilling flavor. It's usually done in oil in a hot pan on the stove. The meat is left on just long enough to brown before being removed

Grilling

Grilling is a great way to finish meat since it adds the smoky flavor and the grill marks so common in grilled foods. For most foods it and pan frying are interchangeable.

Torching

Many people that use sous vide often will invest in a good butane food torch for searing their food. A common torch is the Iwatani torch.

Roasting

Roasting isn't as common as the other methods but it can be a great way to finish crusts or sear the top and sides of sous vide meat. It is normally done at 450°F or under the broiler. You can also do this on your grill by using very high, indirect heat.

Smoking

Some recipes call for food to be smoked either before or after you grill them. You can still accomplish this by smoking it after you remove the food from the sous vide bath. For longer times or cold smoking it can be better to smoke the meat beforehand to minimize the time the food is in the danger zone.

Putting it All Together

Now that you know all the steps it is very easy to take a recipe you love and convert it to a sous vide recipe

Just determine the type of meat being cooked and what recipe method you will use to cook it. Next isolate the seasonings and see if they need to be added before or after the sous vide cooking. Finally, choose your finishing method, usually pan frying or grilling but it can also be roasting or smoking.

Season your food before if it is needed. Place it in the water bath for the indicated time at the indicated temperature. Remove it from the water bath and add any post-bath seasonings. Then finish it with the method of your choice.

SOUS VIDE TIPS

For more tips and tricks you can visit our sous vide forums.
There are a lot of questions answered and information exchanged there.

You can find them on our website here:
www.cookingsousvide.com/sous-vide-forums

FLAVOR

Do Not Salt Before Sous Viding

We recommend only salting your food after they are done sous viding, this is especially important for red meats that are cooked for longer periods of time or where the cook, chill, and hold process is used. The salt begins to cure the meat resulting in less juicy meat at the end.

Always Salt and Pepper After Cooking

While you usually do not want to salt before sous viding, once you remove it from the sous vide bags it is a good idea to salt it before searing it. It's recommended for almost every dish to add salt and pepper before you sear it. Don't be afraid to taste your dishes as they come together to make sure they are properly seasoned. Since the food is already cooked after the sous vide process you can cut off a small piece before searing it to test for seasonings.

Easy on the Spices

Because of the length of time sous vide cooking requires, especially for the tough cuts of meat, and the effects of the vacuum seal, spices can come across much stronger than they would in a normal piece of meat. It's better to err of the side of less and re-season after taking them out of the sous vide bath than to try and eat a dish that only tastes like garlic.

Ingredients, Ingredients, Ingredients

You want to know what the secret to good cooking is? Use high-quality ingredients. The better the ingredients you use the better your resulting dish will be. This is even easier with sous vide since you will be perfectly cooking the food every time and don't have to worry about ruining it.

More and more farmers markets are opening up in cities everywhere and if you are planning a nice meal then the extra flavor from locally grown fruits and vegetables (and even meat) is more than worth the extra money.

Fresh is Better

Another way to improve your dishes is to be sure to use fresh ingredients. If a recipe calls for lime juice or orange juice, instead of using bottled juice just grab a lime and juice it for the recipe, you'll be able to taste the difference.

Turn to the Powders

Using fresh herbs and spices instead of dried ones is normally a good idea when cooking. However, with sous vide it can be better to use the dried powders in some cases. This is especially true for things like garlic, onion, and ginger because the raw form of both can sometimes create a bitterness in the final dish.

Throw Out Your Mops

When you finish sous vide meals you can apply spice rubs or glazes before you finish them on the grill. However, mop sauces and basting sauces don't work well since they prevent the meat from browning and will lead to overcooked meat. To use your favorite sauces I suggest putting a small amount of them into the sous vide pouch with the food before you sous vide it. This is a great way to get the flavor to permeate throughout the meat. One caveat though, be careful with alcohol or vinegar based mops because no evaporation will occur in the pouch. Feel free to experiment with different types and quantities to see what works best for you.

All Meat is Different

More and more people are purchasing meat from places other than the supermarket for a variety of reasons from better flavor and texture to healthier meat and more humane treatment. I'll save any lectures for another time but one thing is apparent, meat raised in different ways behaves differently when cooked. We've found that some grass-fed beef roasts only need to be cooked for about one half the time of a comparable supermarket roast before they become tender. So be aware that meat from different places cooks differently because there's nothing worse than turning an expensive cut of meat to mush.

Give it Some Smoke

If you are preparing a BBQ-style dish it can help if you smoke the meat before sealing it. Even 30-60 minutes in the smoker can add a lot of flavor to the final dish. It's normally better to smoke the food before cooking it as opposed to afterwards because it reduces safety concerns.

Cheat on the Smoke

If you don't have a smoker or the time to smoke your food there is a quicker way to add some smokiness. You can just add a small amount of Liquid Smoke to the bag prior to sealing it. A smoking gun can also be a very useful tool.

Another quick way to add post-sous vide smoke flavor is to add wood chips to your grill to create smoke. When you sear off your sous vide meat this smoke will help flavor it. It won't be a super strong smoke taste but it will definitely add some great flavor.

Remove the Fat

Since sous vide cooking does not get up to high temperatures, about 145°F to 150°F at the most for meats, it does not render fat nearly as well as other cooking techniques. When it comes to dishes cooked over a long period of time, such as short ribs or a roast, be sure to remove any extra fat from the meat before cooking it. This will result in a much leaner and more tender meat with a lot better texture.

SEALING

Don't Stuff the Pouches

In order to ensure proper cooking it's important to make sure the thickness of the food in your pouches is relatively even. Don't force in extra food or layer the food in the pouches. It's better to use multiple pouches with a single layer of food than one large pouch. Most recipes assume a single layer of food when determining the cooking time.

Airtight Ziplocs Using the Displacement Method

If you are using ziploc bags to seal your food you can use this trick to force out the majority of the air. Once it is ready to close, seal all but 1" of the bag. Place the bag into the water bath, making sure to keep that last 1" out of the water. The water will force the remaining air out of the bag and then you can seal it completely. When done properly this is almost as good as using a weak vacuum sealer and will work great for most low-temperature sous vide cooking.

Freeze the Liquids

If you need to seal liquids using your vacuum sealer one easy method is to freeze the liquids first. Then you can add them to the sous vide pouch and seal it. Once the food is in the water bath the liquid will unfreeze and work its magic. Two things to remember: 1) alcohol won't freeze and 2) if there is a large amount of liquid the seal on the bag won't be very tight because liquids are more dense than ice.

Low Temperature + Liquid = Ziplocs

If you need to seal liquid in a sous vide pouch and you are cooking it at a low temperature, the easiest thing to do is to use ziploc bags as the pouch. Using the Airtight Ziplocs tip you can get almost as good of a vacuum as you will be able to with a conventional vacuum sealer and avoid any potential mess.

Need Liquids? Use the Override

Many vacuum sealers have an override switch to seal the bag at its current vacuum state. If you need to seal liquids in the sous vide pouch and you are using a high-temperature dish or you don't want to use ziplocs then you can use this to remove a lot of air from the sous vide pouches.

Fill the sous vide pouch with the food and liquid. Place it in your vacuum sealer and then hang it off of a counter, so the liquid is as far away from the sealer as possible. Be sure to support the bottom of the bag so you don't have a mess on your hands. Then begin the vacuuming process, watching the level of the liquid. As soon as the liquid nears the top of the sous vide pouch hit the

"Seal" button, which should seal the pouch without pulling the liquid all the way out.

FINISHING

Don't Forget the Spice Rubs

Just because your food was already cooked with sous vide doesn't mean you have to omit spice rubs. Once the food is out of the sous vide bath and dried off you can add any of your favorite spice rubs to it. Once you add the spice rub just grill the food as specified and it should turn out great.

Drier the Better

You want meat to be as dry as possible when trying to brown it after sous viding. When it is dry it speeds up the browning process which reduces the amount of extra cooking that occurs.

The easiest way to accomplish this is to use paper towels or a dish towel to pat the meat dry. This also works when cooking raw meat that has been in a marinade. I have specially colored dish towels that I only use for this purpose and wash after each use.

Crank the Heat

When searing foods that have already been cooked sous vide you want to minimize the amount of time they are on the heat. Get your grill as hot as it can go or your pan to the point where the oil just starts to smoke. Only cook the meat until a crust develops or it begins to get grill marks, no more than 1 or 2 minutes per side.

Always Preheat Before Searing

Whether you are finishing your sous vide meat on a grill, on a stove, or in the oven under the broiler you should always preheat it. Putting the meat in a cold pan just takes longer to sear and further cooks the inside of the meat. Using only preheated cooking surfaces helps keep the cooking to the outside of the meat, leaving the inside perfectly cooked.

Oil Can Help With Searing

If you are searing in a pan it can help to add a little bit of oil to help facilitate searing. It also means the meat will not stick, something that can be a problem with the shorter cooking times. This is true on grills as well.

Paint on the Glaze

Another great way to add flavor is to apply a glaze to the food when you put it on the grill or under the broiler. Just add it to the food before you apply the heat and make sure to flip it once or twice so the glaze can take.

GENERAL TIME SAVING TIPS

Cut and Store Vegetables

Cutting vegetables on days you have time is a great way to cut down your prep time on the days you are going to eat. You can wash, peel, and cut most vegetables several days ahead of time and store them in the refrigerator. You can also freeze them in 1 cup portions for several months. Most frozen vegetables do not need to be thawed and can just be added directly to the dishes during cooking.

Blanch and Freeze Vegetables

You can also save time by blanching your vegetables ahead of time and refrigerating or freezing them. To blanch them you just place them in salted, boiling water for several minutes until they begin to become tender. Remove them from the boiling water

and chill them in an ice bath. Dry them off and freeze in plastic bags in 1 cup portions. When it is time to cook you can add them directly to the dish during cooking without thawing.

Freeze Roasted Vegetables

The chill and freeze process also works well for roasted vegetables. You can first roast the vegetables in the oven, let them cook, and then freeze them in a plastic bag in 1 cup portions until you are ready to use them. Most frozen vegetables do not need to be thawed and can just be added directly to the dishes during cooking.

Use Pre-Cut Vegetables

I always stress trying to use fresh, high quality ingredients but sometimes you just don't have the time in the middle of the week. Using pre-cut or pre-shredded vegetables is a great way to shave time off your cooking. Many grocery stores carry already cut vegetables that you can quickly cook in a pan before dinner for a fast and healthy side.

Use Frozen Vegetables

These days you can find almost any vegetable you want in your freezer section. While they might not be as good as produce picked up fresh from a farmers market they are great for middle of the week meals when you need some veggies. When it is time to cook you can add them directly to the dish during cooking without thawing.

Canned Corn is Instant Flavor

Many recipes call for cooked corn kernels and using canned corn is a quick way to get this done. Just use what you need and store the rest of the corn in the refrigerator. You can always grill or roast fresh corn but using canned corn is a great way to do it when pressed for time.

Use Spice Mixtures

There are many different pre-made spice mixtures available at the store and they are a great way to add variety to your meals without creating additional work. You can add the spice before sous viding or before searing and it can transform a plain piece of meat into something exotic.

Store Your Own Mixes

Pre-made spice mixtures are normally pretty good but it can be fun making your own so you can create the exact flavors you want. If you have a favorite spice mix try to double or triple the recipe and store the remaining mixture in a small tupperware container in your cabinet for up to 6 months. It's a great way to enjoy your favorite flavors without having to work as much when you make the food.

Use Bottled Sauces

Bottled sauces are a great way to add flavor and turn a dish into something exotic. Sauces run the gamut from a simple BBQ sauce to Asian stir-fry sauces and Indian curry sauces found in most supermarket "ethnic" aisles. Usually the sauce can be added after the food is removed from the sous vide bath and has been seared. They are also great to use in stir-fries or rice dishes for quickly added flavor.

Store Your Own Sauces

If you enjoy making your own sauces, a great time saving technique is to make extra sauce and freeze it. Most sauce will last for several months without losing any flavor. To freeze the sauce make sure it has cooled off and then divide into ½-1 cup portions.

Alternatively you can pour enough into to a ziploc bag that when laid flat is less than ½" (13mm) thick. Be sure it is flat when it freezes and then you can break off chunks when you need to use it later.

Use Flavored Oils

For more subtle flavor than the sometimes overpowering sauces you can use flavored oils. These come in a variety of flavors from basil to hot chile pepper and can be simply drizzled on top of cooked meat to add richness and flavor. They go especially well with many types of fish.

Use Canned Beans

There is always an argument about whether canned beans are perfect substitutes for fresh beans. However, there is no doubt that using canned beans is much faster. Adding beans is a great way to introduce more heartiness to meals without adding much fat.

Buy Bulk Meat

One great tip for saving time and money is to buy your meat in bulk. You can then take an hour on the weekend to portion and season all the meat and put it in the refrigerator or freezer. During the week you can just grab a pouch and put it into the water bath without having to spend any extra time.

Freeze Meats into Portions

If you plan on buying larger quantities of meat and then storing them it can be a nice time saver if you freeze them in the portion sizes you will need. If you store them in sizes of around a pound they can be easy to add to any recipe. We have found very little reduction in food quality from freezing foods.

Season After the Sous Vide

Many sous vide recipes call for meat to be cooked with spices but if you don't have the time beforehand you can still add a lot of flavor after the fact. Salsas, pan sauces, BBQ sauce, and Asian sauces are all great ways to quickly add flavor to a dish at the end of the cooking time.

Use Meat Straight from Freezer

Meat that is frozen heats up very quickly and only adds about 20% to the heating time shown in the "Cooking by Thickness" section. Taking your pre-seasoned and portioned meat directly out of the freezer can save you time and planning while still following the cooking ranges.

You Can Skip the Pre-Seasonings

While each recipe has suggestions for seasoning before you sous vide the meat it's not always necessary. If you pre-package your meat you might not know what it will be used for and many times it is fine to skip the pre-seasoning step. There will be some flavor loss but the gain in time can be more than worth it.

Pre-Cook Pasta and Rice

An easy way to create fast meals during the week is to cook large quantities of pasta or rice and freeze them. They will last for several months and can be quickly reheated on the day you want to use them in a meal.

ABOUT THE RECIPES

We are constantly adding recipes to our website as we continue to experiment with sous vide. Maybe something there will inspire you.

You can find them at:
www.cookingsousvide.com/info/sous-vide-recipes

Here are some general guidelines about our recipes.

Read the Recipe FIRST

This might sound like a no-brainer but with sous vide it is very important to read the whole recipe before starting. Many recipes require marinades or other initial steps and often times you need to start working on the finishing portion of the recipe while the meat is still cooking. Just read through the recipe first, make sure you understand it, and then you won't run into any surprises down the road.

Choose the Best Method for You

Just because a recipe is in the Day Of section doesn't mean you can't chill and hold it. The recipe sections are set up to illustrate how the different methods work but many of the recipes are interchangeable and you can change them by following the steps in another method. Use the methods as a way to help plan your meals around your schedule.

Choose Your Own Temperature

Our recipes just give you a single temperature and a time range for each dish. The temperatures are based on our personal preferences and are usually on the medium-rare side. If you prefer food cooked more or less you can refer to our comprehensive *Time and Temperature Charts* for the cut of meat used in that dish.

Sous Vide Pouches

In the recipes we just say "Add the food to the sous vide pouches". This can be any type of sous vide pouch you feel comfortable using, from plastic wrap or ziplocs up to industrial food pouches.

It also assumes that you are using as many sous vide pouches as you need for the food to lay in one even layer, usually less than 2" thick. If spices or liquids are added to the pouches then just split them evenly between all the pouches.

Use Oil for Better Searing

In the recipes we don't specify whether or not to use oil for searing since some people feel strongly about searing in a dry pan. We personally like using oil since it seems to brown faster and the food doesn't stick. We like canola oil for its higher smoking point.

If you'd like to use oil just add a thin film of it to the pan and let it just begin to shimmer and smoke before adding the food to be seared.

Salt and Pepper

Most of the recipes call for "Salt and pepper" as an ingredient. Proper seasoning is critical to good cooking and you should salt and pepper your ingredients after they come out of the pouches as you are searing them and making any finishing steps.

While we'd like to give you specific measurements, how much you use is in large part a matter of taste. And since studies show this likely differs across people through genetics and upbringing, we haven't given specifics. Be sure to taste your food as you go and you should be fine.

Mix and Match Recipes

Many of the sides, spices, and salsas can go with a variety of meats. If a dish sounds good but you have flank steak on hand instead of sirloin steak go ahead and switch them.

You can also apply recipes to other cuts of meat in the same way, like taking a steak recipe and using it for chicken. Just find the cut of meat you'd like to use in the *Time and Temperature Charts* and use the values given there instead of the ones in the recipe. Feel free to experiment with the meats to see what combinations you prefer.

Substitutions are Great

Just because a recipe calls for an ingredient doesn't mean you have to use it. Feel free to leave out spices you don't like (or use less of them), add in your favorite vegetables, use a different sauce, or just use the recipe as a general guideline and create your own dish. Cooking should be fun and experimenting with the ingredients is part of the joy.

Working Times Are Relative

We provide both Pre-Bath and Finishing times for all recipes. Times are hard to come up with because a professional chef can prepare food much faster than my Grandma. In general we tried to use times for a "normal" home cook. We also did our best to be consistent across recipes. So while it might take you longer or shorter than the times say, it should be that way for all recipes and you can use them as a general guideline.

Boneless vs Bone-In

Many ingredients come either with or without the bone in them. We usually don't specify which version to use for a dish because often both work well. Just make sure if the bone is sharp you don't vacuum seal it too tightly or it could puncture the pouch.

One exception to this is for sandwiches, in which case you should use the boneless version or at least remove the bone before putting it together.

Fish Doesn't Mean Whole Fish

Unless otherwise specified when we say "1 pound mahi mahi" we are referring to filets or steaks, not whole fish. Whole fish can be done sous vide but are not covered here. We're assuming filets or steaks ½" to 1" thick.

DAY OF MEATS

You can stay up to date with the current happenings in sous vide by reading our blog. We try to update it regularly with current information about sous vide.

You can find it at:
www.cookingsousvide.com/info/sous-vide-blog

General Process

Day Of recipes focus on foods that you can cook during a typical work day. You put the food in before you leave in the morning and when you get home 8 to 12 hours later it will be completely cooked. You just need to finish the meal and sear the meat.

Pre-Bath Stage

The *Pre-Bath* stage usually will consist of seasoning and bagging the food. Unless you need to cube or trim the meat it is a very quick process. Even so, unless you're a morning person we don't recommend doing this in the morning.

You have two other options which can be done at potentially better and less stressful times. First, you can do it up to two days beforehand and refrigerate it. Or second, you can do it several months ahead of time and freeze it. Either way, on the day you want to cook you can just toss the pouch in the water bath without adding work to your morning.

Cooking Stage

The *Cooking* stage will usually last for 8 to 12 hours and should be timed so it ends when you will want to eat later in the day. We also include chicken and pork chops which are more moist when cooked for shorter amounts of time but still taste great at the longer times.

You can also use any of these recipes using the cook, chill, and hold technique.

Finishing Stage

The *Finishing* stage will generally be completed right after you remove the food from the water bath. For most recipes you take the meat out of the pouch, pat it dry, and sear it. You also make any sides or salsas as well as make any side dishes or sauces for it.

Common Day Of Meats

Here are some of the more common meats that can be cooked during a single day in the 8 to 12 hour time frame.

Beef Roasts

Prime Rib: 5-10 hours
Rib Eye: 5-10 hours
Sirloin Roast: 5-10 hours
Stew Meat: 4-8 hours
Tri-Tip Roast: 5-10 hours

Beef Steaks

Blade: 4-10 hours
Flank: 2-12 hours
Flat Iron: 4-10 hours
Sirloin: 2-10 hours
Tri-Tip Steak: 2-10 hours

Chicken

Shredding: 8-12 hours
Thighs and breasts: 3-12 hours, they are better cooked for 2 to 4 hours but still good for this long

Pork

Baby Back Ribs: 8-10 hours
Back Ribs: 8-10 hours
Blade Chops: 8-12 hours
Chops: 3-12 hours, they are better cooked for 3 to 6 hours but still good for this long
Country Style Ribs: 8-12 hours
Ham Roast: 10-20 hours
Shank: 8-10 hours
Sirloin Chops: 6-12 hours
Sirloin Roast: 6-12 hours

Tips and Tricks

Bag It Ahead of Time

Mornings have a tendency to be hectic so we recommend not trying to prep your food the day you are cooking it. There's nothing worse than adding more stress to your day right off the bat.

Either prep and bag your food a few days earlier and keep it in the refrigerator or do it weeks in advance and keep it in the freezer. That way you just have to toss the bag into the water bath on your way out the door.

Cook at a Lower Temperature

For some meats like chicken and pork, the longer cooking times can dry the meat out some. I recommend cooking these at the lower temperatures (135°F / 57°C for pork, 141°F / 60.5°C for chicken) since they will dry out less.

If you prefer them cooked at a higher temperature you can either sear them for longer on the grill, or turn up the water bath to the desired temperature when you get home since it will only take a short time to raise the food the final few degrees.

TUSCAN PRIME RIB

Pre-Bath Time: 15 Minutes
Cooking Time: 5 to 10 Hours
Finishing Time: 15 Minutes
Temperature: 131°F / 55°C
Serves: 4 to 8

Pre-Bath Ingredients
3 pounds prime rib roast

For the Rub
¼ cup fresh rosemary
¼ cup fresh parsley
3 tablespoons fresh oregano
2 tablespoons fresh sage
2 garlic cloves, coarsely chopped
2 tablespoons black pepper
½ cup olive oil

Finishing Ingredients
No ingredients

This recipe uses bold herbs to add a lot of flavor to a savory prime rib roast cut. The herbs really infuse the meal during the cooking time and deepen the flavor. Some people don't like fresh herbs in sous vide so you can substitute dried herbs if you prefer.

The roast is great with the Savory Asparagus, Broccoli Raab with Hot Peppers, or the Garlic Sauteed Mushrooms.

Pre-Bath
To make the Tuscan rub, put all of the rub ingredients into a food processor and process until mixed.

Rub the roast with the Tuscan rub and place in the sous vide pouch. Seal the pouch.

At this point you can store the pouch in the refrigerator for up to 2 days, freeze it for up to 6 months, or cook it right away.

Cooking
On the morning of the day you want to eat, preheat your sous vide water bath to 131°F / 55°C. Place the pouch in the water bath for 5 to 10 hours.

Finishing
Preheat a grill or pan to very hot.

Take the roast out of the water bath and remove it from the pouch. Pat it dry with a paper towel or dish cloth. Quickly sear for 1 to 2 minutes per side, just until browned.

Take the roast off the heat and serve as you would a normal roast. I like to slice it very thinly or into ½" slabs.

BBQ Tri-Tip Steaks

Pre-Bath Time: 15 Minutes
Cooking Time: 5 to 10 Hours
Finishing Time: 15 Minutes
Temperature: 131°F / 55°C
Serves: 4 to 8

Pre-Bath Ingredients

For the Steaks
3 pound Tri-Tip Roast, cut into 1½" slabs
2 tablespoons garlic powder
2-4 rosemary sprigs
2-4 thyme sprigs
Pepper

Finishing Ingredients

⅔ cup BBQ sauce

We convert a tri tip roast to steaks in this recipe which is a great way to use a less expensive cut of meat to get great steaks. We add BBQ sauce, garlic, and rosemary for extra flavor but you can use any seasonings you prefer.

You can serve this meal with mashed potatoes or our Mushrooms with Brandy-Cream sauce.

Pre-Bath

Pepper the meat then sprinkle with the garlic powder. Add it to the sous vide pouches with the rosemary and thyme sprigs then seal.

At this point you can store the pouch in the refrigerator for up to 2 days, freeze it for up to 6 months, or cook it right away.

Cooking

On the morning of the day you want to eat, preheat your sous vide water bath to 131°F / 55°C. Place the pouch in the water bath for 5 to 10 hours.

Finishing

Preheat a grill to high or a pan to medium-high.

Take the beef slabs out of the water bath and remove them from the pouches. Pat them dry with a paper towel or dish cloth. Quickly sear the slabs for 1 to 2 minutes per side. Brush both sides with the BBQ sauce and cook for 30 seconds on each side.

Take the beef off the heat and serve.

STEAK WITH SPRING SALSA

Pre-Bath Time: 10 Minutes
Cooking Time: 2 to 10 Hours
Finishing Time: 30 Minutes
Temperature: 131°F / 55°C
Serves: 4

Pre-Bath Ingredients
For the Steak
1-2 pounds sirloin steak
1 teaspoon dried thyme
1 teaspoon cumin powder
Pepper

Finishing Ingredients
For the Salsa
1 cup cherry tomatoes, halved
5 radishes, diced
1 cup corn kernels, cooked
¼ red onion, diced
¼ cup chopped fresh basil
1 tablespoon white wine vinegar
2 tablespoons olive oil
Salt and pepper

This spring salsa is very simple to make and really adds some lightness and flavor to the dish. It's great in late spring when the cherry tomatoes are just starting to ripen. It also goes well with chicken or turkey breasts.

Pre-Bath
Pepper the meat then sprinkle with the cumin and thyme. Add to the sous vide pouches and seal.

At this point you can store the pouch in the refrigerator for up to 2 days, freeze it for up to 6 months, or cook it right away.

Cooking
On the morning of the day you want to eat, preheat your sous vide water bath to 131°F / 55°C. Place the pouch in the water bath for 2 to 10 hours.

Finishing
Preheat a grill to high heat or a pan to medium-high heat.

To make the salsa mix all of the ingredients in a bowl. It's best to make the salsa right before you take the steaks out of the water bath.

Take the steaks out of the pouches and pat dry. Sear them until just browned, about 1 to 2 minutes per side. Place the steaks on a plate and top with a spoonful or two of the salsa.

BEEF WITH ORANGE SAUCE

Pre-Bath Time: 10 Minutes
Cooking Time: 2 to 10 Hours
Finishing Time: 30 Minutes
Temperature: 131°F / 55°C
Serves: 4

Pre-bath Ingredients
For the Steak
1½ pound sirloin steak
1 teaspoon garlic powder
½ teaspoon ginger powder
Pepper

Finishing Ingredients
For the Sauce
2 cups mandarin oranges
3 tablespoons sesame oil
3 scallions, thinly sliced
1 tablespoon garlic, minced
1 tablespoon fresh ginger, minced
1½ cups orange juice
2 tablespoons soy sauce
2 tablespoons honey
Salt and pepper
4 tablespoons cold water
4 tablespoons corn starch

For Garnish
½ tablespoon grated orange peel
½ cup chopped fresh parsley
4 cups cooked white rice

Orange beef can be found at many Chinese restaurants. This is my take on it with an eye for making it fast. The grated orange peel adds some flavor without overpowering it. To zest the orange you can use a microplane or the small holes on a grater.

This sauce is also very good with chicken, pork, or even swordfish steaks. For an even fuller meal you can add steamed broccoli, mushrooms, snap peas, or other vegetables to it.

Pre-Bath
Mix the spices together in a small bowl. Pepper the steak and sprinkle with the spices. Put it into the sous vide pouch and seal.

At this point you can store the pouch in the refrigerator for up to 2 days, freeze it for up to 6 months, or cook it right away.

Cooking
On the morning of the day you want to eat, preheat your sous vide water bath to 131°F / 55°C. Place the pouch in the water bath for 2 to 10 hours.

Finishing
Heat a pan over medium heat for the sauce and one over medium-high heat to sear the steaks.

About 10 minutes before the steaks are done start on the sauce.

Add the oil and scallions to the pan over medium heat and cook for 1 to 2 minutes. Add the garlic and ginger and cook for 1 to 2 minutes more. Add the orange juice, soy sauce, honey, salt, and pepper, and a quarter of the Mandarin oranges. Cook until it thickens slightly, about 5 minutes, and the flavors are combined. Remove from the heat and keep warm.

Remove the steak from the sous vide bath and pat dry. Sear it until browned, 1 to 2 minutes per side. Remove from the heat and cut into bite-size pieces.

Add some of the juices from the bag to the orange sauce and bring to a simmer. Mix together the corn starch and cold water then gradually whisk into the sauce until it thickens to your desired consistency, the more of the water and corn starch mixture you add the thicker it will get. Stir the steak pieces and orange segments into the sauce and warm throughout.

Put a large spoonful of white rice on a plate or in a bowl and top with the beef and orange mixture. Sprinkle with the orange peel and parsley then serve.

SIRLOIN STEAK WITH HERBED BUTTER

Pre-Bath Time: 10 Minutes
Cooking Time: 2 to 10 Hours
Finishing Time: 30 Minutes
Temperature: 131°F / 55°C
Serves: 4

Pre-Bath Ingredients
For the Steak
1-2 pounds sirloin steak
1 teaspoon dried thyme
1 teaspoon cumin powder
Pepper

Finishing Ingredients
For the Butter
½ stick butter, softened at room temperature
1 tablespoon finely chopped fresh parsley
1 tablespoon finely chopped fresh basil
1 tablespoon finely chopped fresh tarragon
⅛ teaspoon ground black pepper

The herbs in this butter add some lightness to the dish while the butter adds richness. You can substitute for any of the herbs and try out other combinations you like.

Note: You can save extra time by doubling or tripling the butter recipe and storing the extra in the freezer where it will last several months. A good way to store it is to roll it up into a cylinder shape with wax paper. You can then just cut off a disk when you want to use it.

Pre-Bath
Pepper the steaks then sprinkle with the cumin and thyme. Add to the sous vide pouches then seal.

At this point you can store the pouch in the refrigerator for up to 2 days, freeze it for up to 6 months, or cook it right away.

Cooking
On the morning of the day you want to eat, preheat your sous vide water bath to 131°F / 55°C. Place the pouch in the water bath for 2 to 10 hours.

Finishing
Preheat a grill to high heat or a pan to medium-high heat.

To make the butter place all of the ingredients in a bowl and mix and mash thoroughly using a fork.

Take the steaks out of the pouches and pat dry. Sear them until just browned, about 1 to 2 minutes per side.

Place the steaks on a plate and top with a dollop or two of the butter.

GRILLED FLAT IRON WITH RASPBERRY SALAD

Pre-Bath Time: 10 Minutes
Cooking Time: 4 to 10 Hours
Finishing Time: 30 Minutes
Temperature: 131°F / 55°C
Serves: 2

Pre-Bath Ingredients
For the Steak
1 pound flat iron steak
½ teaspoon garlic powder
¼ teaspoon thyme powder
Pepper

Finishing Ingredients
For the Dressing
2 tablespoons raspberry or raspberry champagne
   vinegar
1 tablespoon orange juice
1 shallot, diced
2 tablespoons honey
5 tablespoons olive oil
Salt and pepper

For the Salad
Mixed baby greens or the lettuce of your choice
½ yellow or red bell pepper, diced
10 cherry tomatoes, halved
¼ cup fresh raspberries or mixed berries
2 radishes, sliced
2 tablespoons sunflower seeds

This is a nice and light steak salad that will fill you up without making you stuffed. It uses a raspberry vinaigrette but you can use any light dressing you have on hand. The fresh berries give it a nice sweet and sour note.

Grilling the steak after the sous vide also adds additional bold flavors to the salad but it can be pan seared if you prefer. If you can't find raspberry vinegar you can use white or red wine vinegar.

Pre-Bath
Prepare the meat by trimming off any excess fat. Pepper the meat then sprinkle with the garlic and thyme. Place in the sous vide pouch and seal.

At this point you can store the pouch in the refrigerator for up to 2 days, freeze it for up to 6 months, or cook it right away.

Cooking
On the morning of the day you want to eat, preheat your sous vide water bath to 131°F / 55°C. Place the pouch in the water bath for 4 to 10 hours.

Finishing
Preheat a grill to very hot.

Make the dressing by whisking together the vinegar, orange juice, shallot, and honey. Slowly whisk in the olive oil until it comes together. Salt and pepper to taste.

Remove the steak from the sous vide pouch and path dry. Sear it until just browned, about 1 to 2 minutes per side. Remove from the heat and slice into short strips.

Assemble the salad by placing the lettuce on plates. Top with the pepper, tomatoes, raspberries, and radishes. Drizzle the vinaigrette on the salad and add the strips of steak. Top with the sunflower seeds. Lightly sprinkle the salad with salt and pepper and serve.

FLANK STEAK WITH SALSA VERDE

Pre-Bath Time: 15 Minutes
Cooking Time: 2 to 12 Hours
Finishing Time: 30 Minutes
Temperature: 131°F / 55°C
Serves: 4 to 6

Pre-Bath Ingredients
For the Steak
1-2 pounds flank steak
1 teaspoon dried thyme
1 teaspoon cumin powder
Pepper

Finishing Ingredients
For the Salsa Verde
8-10 tomatillos, coarsely chopped
½ cup fresh cilantro
1 shallot, coarsely chopped
3 garlic cloves, coarsely chopped
1 jalapeno pepper, deseeded and coarsely
    chopped
1 tablespoon lime juice
1 tablespoon olive oil
Salt and pepper

Salsa verde adds a nice tang to complement the beefiness of the flank steak and is very easy to put together. For another take on this dish you can first roast or grill the tomatillos and jalapeno before making the salsa. This dish is complemented nicely by refried beans and yellow rice.

Note: I prefer my flank steak to have some bite to it so I normally cook it for 2 to 12 hours but some people prefer it to be meltingly tender and cook it for 1 to 2 days. If you want to try that then start it in the water bath 1 to 2 days before you want to eat.

Pre-Bath
Pepper the meat then sprinkle with the cumin and thyme. Add to the sous vide pouches and seal.

At this point you can store the pouch in the refrigerator for up to 2 days, freeze it for up to 6 months, or cook it right away.

Cooking
On the morning of the day you want to eat, preheat your sous vide water bath to 131°F / 55°C. Place the pouch in the water bath for 2 to 12 hours.

Finishing
Preheat a grill to high heat or a pan to medium-high heat.

To make the salsa place all of the salsa ingredients in a food processor and process until it blends together. It's best to make the salsa right before you take the steaks out of the water bath.

Take the steaks out of the pouches and pat dry. Sear them until just browned, about 1 to 2 minutes per side. Cut the steak into ¼" to ½" strips and place on a plate. Top with a spoonful or two of the salsa verde.

Steak Quesadillas

Pre-Bath Time: 15 Minutes
Cooking Time: 2 to 10 Hours
Finishing Time: 30 to 45 Minutes
Temperature: 131°F / 55°C
Serves: 4

Pre-Bath Ingredients
For the Steak
1 pound sirloin steak
1 teaspoon paprika
½ teaspoon garlic powder
½ teaspoon ground cumin
½ teaspoon fennel seeds
½ teaspoon dry mustard powder
Pepper

Finishing Ingredients
For the Quesadillas
8 flour tortillas
2 cups shredded cheddar cheese
1 cup shredded munster cheese
1 poblano pepper, thinly sliced
1 sweet onion, thinly sliced
½ cup chopped watercress
1 tomato, diced
¼ cup cooked corn kernels

Canola or olive oil

Quesadillas are a great way to use up different meats and vegetables you have around the house. They are very fast to put together and precooking the steak with sous vide means it stays very moist. Feel free to substitute any cheeses you prefer and to have fun playing around with the ingredients.

For more flavor you can grill or roast the onion and poblano pepper before adding to the quesadillas.

Pre-Bath
Mix the spices together in a bowl. Pepper the steak then sprinkle with the spice mixture and seal in a sous vide pouch.

At this point you can store the pouch in the refrigerator for up to 2 days, freeze it for up to 6 months, or cook it right away.

Cooking
On the morning of the day you want to eat, preheat your sous vide water bath to 131°F / 55°C. Place the pouch in the water bath for 2 to 10 hours.

Finishing
Preheat a grill to high heat or a pan to medium-high heat.

Remove the steak from the water bath and cut into ½" strips.

Lay out 4 tortillas and evenly split the steak and other ingredients between them. Top each with a remaining tortilla.

Brush the top of each tortilla with oil and place on the grill or in the pan. Cover the tortilla while it is cooking. Once it turns golden brown on the bottom flip it over and continue cooking until the cheese is melted and the quesadilla is browned on both side.

Remove from the heat, cut into quarters, and serve.

FLANK STEAK WITH SAUTEED VEGETABLES

Pre-Bath Time: 15 Minutes
Cooking Time: 2 to 12 Hours
Finishing Time: 45 Minutes
Temperature: 131°F / 55°C
Serves: 4 to 6

Pre-Bath Ingredients

For the Steak
1-2 pounds flank steak
1 teaspoon dried thyme
1 teaspoon ground coriander
½ teaspoon ancho chile powder or chile powder
  of your choice
Pepper

Finishing Ingredients

For the Vegetables
2 tablespoons canola oil
1 onion, thickly sliced
1 zucchini, cut into ½" slices
2 tablespoons butter
12 ounces baby bella mushrooms, thickly sliced
2 tablespoons balsamic vinegar
¼ cup chopped fresh basil
Salt and pepper

These sauteed vegetables are a healthy way to add some heft to this meal and they complement the beefiness of the steak. The balsamic vinegar adds a nice tang and sweetness without overpowering the dish. I prefer to use baby bella mushrooms but white button mushrooms will also work fine. You can also use any vegetables you have on hand including yellow squash, asparagus, carrots, or bell peppers.

Note: I prefer my flank steak to have some bite to it so I normally cook it for 2 to 12 hours but some people prefer it to be meltingly tender and cook it for 1 to 2 days. If you want to try that then start it in the water bath 1 to 2 days before you want to eat.

Pre-Bath

Mix the spices together in a bowl. Pepper the meat then sprinkle with the spices. Add to the sous vide pouches and seal.

At this point you can store the pouch in the refrigerator for up to 2 days, freeze it for up to 6 months, or cook it right away.

Cooking

On the morning of the day you want to eat, preheat your sous vide water bath to 131°F / 55°C. Place the pouch in the water bath for 2 to 12 hours.

Finishing

Preheat a grill to high heat or a pan to medium-high heat.

Heat the oil in another pan over medium heat. Add the onion and cook until it begins to soften, 5 to 10 minutes. Add the zucchini and cook until it begins to become tender, about 5 minutes. Add the butter and the mushrooms and cook until they soften. Add the vinegar and stir while it reduces. Stir in the basil and remove from the heat.

Take the steaks out of the pouches and pat dry with a paper towel or dish towel. Sear them until just browned, about 1 to 2 minutes per side. Place the steaks on a plate and top with several spoonfuls of the vegetables.

SAVORY SIRLOIN ROAST

Pre-Bath Time: 15 Minutes
Cooking Time: 5 to 10 Hours
Finishing Time: 15 Minutes
Temperature: 131°F / 55°C
Serves: 4

Pre-Bath Ingredients
For the Steak
3-4 pound sirloin roast
1 tablespoon garlic powder
1 tablespoon onion powder
2 teaspoons ground coriander
4 rosemary sprigs
4 thyme sprigs
Pepper

Finishing Ingredients
None

Having a sirloin roast for dinner during the week seems like a huge undertaking but with sous vide it becomes a simple thing to accomplish. All you have to do when you are ready to eat is make any sides you want and then quickly sear the roast. It's a great way to have a traditional family meal during the week without expending any extra effort.

Pre-Bath
Mix the spices together in a bowl. Pepper the meat then sprinkle with the spices. Place in a sous vide pouch with the rosemary and thyme then seal the pouch.

At this point you can store the pouch in the refrigerator for up to 2 days, freeze it for up to 6 months, or cook it right away.

Cooking
On the morning of the day you want to eat, preheat your sous vide water bath to 131°F / 55°C. Place the pouch in the water bath for 5 to 10 hours.

Finishing
Preheat a pan to medium-high heat.

Take the roast out of the sous vide pouch and pat dry. Sear it in the hot pan, about 1 to 2 minutes per side, until just browned.

Slice the roast into serving portions, I prefer either very thin or ½" thick, and serve. You can also serve the juices from the pouch on the side as au jus.

CHICKEN SANDWICH WITH BALSAMIC ONIONS

Pre-Bath Time: 15 Minutes
Cooking Time: 2 to 12 Hours
Finishing Time: 40 Minutes
Temperature: 141°F / 60.5°C
Serves: 4

Pre-Bath Ingredients
For the Chicken
4 chicken breasts
½ teaspoon garlic powder
½ teaspoon onion powder
½ teaspoon ancho chile powder or chile powder
    of your choice
Pepper

Finishing Ingredients
For the Onion
1 onion, thickly sliced
1 tablespoon fresh thyme
1 tablespoon balsamic vinegar

For the Sandwiches
4 sandwich rolls or buns
4 slices swiss cheese

I love the sweet and tart flavor of balsamic onions. They're really easy to make and add a burst of flavor to many different dishes. These chicken sandwiches are great with a side salad or vegetables. Cooking them sous vide ensures that the chicken is very moist.

Note: Usually chicken is best when cooked for 2 to 4 hours but during the week you can get away with cooking it for up to 12 hours with just a minimal loss in moisture.

Pre-Bath
Mix the spices together in a bowl. Pepper the chicken then sprinkle with the spice mixture and seal in sous vide pouches.

At this point you can store the pouch in the refrigerator for up to 2 days, freeze it for up to 6 months, or cook it right away.

Cooking
On the morning of the day you want to eat, preheat your sous vide water bath to 141°F / 60.5°C. Place the pouch in the water bath for 2 to 12 hours.

Finishing
Preheat a grill to high heat or a pan to medium-high heat. Preheat the broiler on the oven.

Heat another over medium heat, add some canola or olive oil and warm. Add the onion and thyme then salt and pepper it. Cook until the onion is soft, about 15 minutes. About 10 minutes into the process add the balsamic vinegar and stir well.

Remove the chicken from the water bath and pat dry. Sear on a hot grill or in a hot pan, about 1 or 2 minutes per side.

Place the chicken on a roasting sheet. Cover the chicken with the onion and top with the cheese. Place the buns on the sheet with the cut side up. Place the whole roasting sheet under the broiler until the cheese melts and the buns begin to brown.

Remove the sheet from the oven, place the chicken in the buns and serve.

CHICKEN THIGHS IN ROASTED TOMATO SALSA

Pre-Bath Time: 15 Minutes
Cooking Time: 2 to 12 Hours
Finishing Time: 45 Minutes
Temperature: 148°F / 64.4°C
Serves: 4

Pre-Bath Ingredients
For the Chicken
6 chicken thighs
1 tablespoon garlic powder
1 teaspoon ancho chile powder, or chile powder
    of your choice
Pepper

Finishing Ingredients
For the Salsa
½ yellow onion, diced
5 large tomatoes, roughly diced
1 tablespoon fresh thyme
5 garlic cloves, diced
2 tablespoons cider vinegar
2 tablespoons brown sugar
¼-1 teaspoon chipotle chile powder, or chile
    powder of your choice

*Salsas are a great way to add flavor to dishes.
Roasting the vegetables first adds even more flavor to
the salsa. Though if you're in a time crunch you can
just use canned tomatoes and it will still turn out
well.*

*Note: Usually chicken thighs are best when cooked for
2 to 5 hours but during the week you can get away
with cooking them for up to 12 hours with just a
minimal loss in moisture.*

Pre-Bath
Trim most of the excess fat off of the thighs.
Pepper them then sprinkle with the garlic
and ancho chile powders. Place the chicken
thighs in the pouches then seal them.

At this point you can store the pouch in the
refrigerator for up to 2 days, freeze it for up
to 6 months, or cook it right away.

Cooking
On the morning of the day you want to eat,
preheat your sous vide water bath to 148°F /
64.4°C. Place the pouch in the water bath for
2 to 12 hours.

Finishing
Preheat the oven to 400°F / 204°C.

Add the onion and tomatoes to a sheet pan
with raised sides then sprinkle with the
thyme and garlic. Cook in the oven until
they soften and begin to brown, 15 to 20
minutes.

Preheat a pan to medium-high heat.

Remove the thighs from the pouch and pat
dry. Sear them in the pan for 1 to 2 minutes
per side, just until browned. Remove from
the heat.

Add the roasted tomato mixture, the cider
vinegar, brown sugar, and chipotle powder
to the pan. Stir while it comes to a simmer.
Remove from the heat and spoon over the
chicken thighs to serve.

CHICKEN PARMIGIANA

Pre-Bath Time: 15 Minutes
Cooking Time: 2 to 12 Hours
Finishing Time: 45 Minutes
Temperature: 141°F / 60.5°C
Serves: 4

Pre-Bath Ingredients

For the Chicken
4 chicken breasts
½ teaspoon garlic powder
4 sprigs fresh thyme
4 sprigs fresh rosemary
Pepper

Finishing Ingredients

For the Coating
¾ cup flour
2 teaspoons salt
1 teaspoon black pepper
2 eggs
¾ cup dried Italian bread crumbs
¼ cup grated parmesan cheese
2 tablespoons chopped parsley

For the Topping
½ cup chopped basil
8-10 ¼" slices of fresh mozzarella, or 1 cup
    shredded
4 tablespoons grated parmesan cheese

Chicken Parmigiana is one of my favorite dishes and I get it at almost every Italian restaurant I go to. Here's a simple version that you can make at home. The sous vide process ensures the chicken is cooked through and you can just focus on getting the coating nice and crispy. I love to serve this with spaghetti and marinara sauce on the side. You can also serve this in a toasted hoagie roll with marinara sauce for a chicken parm grinder, a staple on most New England menus. You can leave the chicken breasts whole or cut them in half width-wise for a higher "crust to chicken" ratio.

Note: Chicken is best when cooked for 2 to 4 hours but during the week you can get away with cooking it for up to 12 hours with just a minimal loss in moisture.

Pre-Bath

Pepper the chicken then sprinkle with the garlic powder. Place in sous vide pouches with the thyme and rosemary and seal.

At this point you can store the pouch in the refrigerator for up to 2 days, freeze it for up to 6 months, or cook it right away.

Cooking

On the morning of the day you want to eat, preheat your sous vide water bath to 141°F / 60.5°C. Place the pouch in the water bath for 2 to 12 hours.

Finishing

Preheat a pan to medium high heat. Preheat the broiler on the oven.

First you will want to set up three stations for the breading. Combine the flour, salt, and pepper on a plate. Beat the eggs into a wide mouth bowl. Combine the bread crumbs, parmesan cheese, and parsley on another plate.

Remove the chicken from the pouches and pat dry. Dredge the chicken in the flour, then the egg, then the bread crumbs.

Add about ½" of oil to the pan and heat to about 350°F to 375°F (176°C - 190°C). Sear the dredged chicken breasts until the crust becomes golden brown, flip and repeat on the other side. Remove from the heat and set on a sheet pan.

Top each one with the basil and cover with the mozzarella and parmesan cheese. Broil in the oven until the cheese is browned and bubbly. Remove and serve.

Classic Chicken Caesar Salad

Pre-Bath Time: 15 Minutes
Cooking Time: 2 to 12 Hours
Finishing Time: 30 Minutes
Temperature: 141°F / 60.5°C
Serves: 6

Pre-Bath Ingredients

For the Chicken
2-3 chicken breasts
1 teaspoon garlic powder
1 teaspoon paprika
½ teaspoon ground cumin
Pepper

Finishing Ingredients

For the Dressing
1 egg yolk
2 anchovy filets
1 teaspoon Dijon mustard
1 teaspoon minced garlic
3 tablespoons fresh lemon juice
½ cup olive oil
Salt and pepper

For the Salad
1 head romaine lettuce, coarsely chopped
½ cup parmesan cheese, freshly grated
2 cups croutons

Caesar salad is a nice and refreshing salad that is made more hardy with the addition of seared chicken. If you worry about the raw egg you can pasteurize it at 135°F for 75 Min (57.2°C) before adding it to the salad.

You can also easily make fresh croutons by dicing bread, drizzling it with olive oil and garlic powder then toasting until it browns.

Note: Usually chicken is best when cooked for 2 to 4 hours but during the week you can get away with cooking it for up to 12 hours with just a minimal loss in moisture.

Pre-Bath

In a small bowl mix together the spices. Season the chicken breasts with the pepper then sprinkle with the spices. Add to the sous vide pouch and seal.

At this point you can store the pouch in the refrigerator for up to 2 days, freeze it for up to 6 months, or cook it right away.

Cooking

On the morning of the day you want to eat, preheat your sous vide water bath to 141°F / 60.5°C. Place the pouch in the water bath for 2 to 12 hours.

Finishing

Heat a pan over medium-high heat.

First make the dressing. Place the egg yolk, anchovies, garlic, mustard, and lemon juice into a food processor and process until thoroughly mixed. With the food processor still running slowly add the oil. Add salt and pepper, tasting until the seasoning is right.

Take the chicken out of the pouch and pat dry. Sear the chicken over high-heat in a hot pan until just browned, about 1 to 2 minutes per side. Remove from the heat and slice.

Place the lettuce in a large bowl. Add enough dressing to coat and toss the lettuce to evenly mix. Place the coated lettuce on individual plates. Top with the chicken, parmesan cheese, and croutons. Crack some fresh pepper on top and serve.

Louisiana Blackened Chicken

Pre-Bath Time: 15 Minutes
Cooking Time: 2 to 12 Hours
Finishing Time: 15 Minutes
Temperature: 141°F / 60.5°C
Serves: 6

Pre-Bath Ingredients
6 chicken breasts

For the Rub
2 tablespoons paprika
2 tablespoons garlic powder
1½ tablespoons onion powder
1 tablespoon cayenne pepper, or to taste
1 tablespoon freshly ground black pepper
1 tablespoon dried oregano
1 tablespoon dried thyme
1 tablespoon dried basil
1 teaspoon white pepper
1 teaspoon ground bay leaf

Finishing Ingredients
None

Blackening chicken or fish adds a ton of flavor to the meat. It's a mixture of many different spices that all bring something to the table. This goes great with red beans and rice or even dirty rice.

Note: Usually chicken is best when cooked for 2 to 4 hours but during the week you can get away with cooking it for up to 12 hours with just a minimal loss in moisture.

Pre-Bath

First make your rub by combining all the ingredients in a bowl and mix well. Any left over rub can be stored in a jar or tupperware container for several months in a cabinet.

Sprinkle the chicken breasts on both sides with half of the rub, place in the sous vide pouches, and seal.

At this point you can store the pouch in the refrigerator for up to 2 days, freeze it for up to 6 months, or cook it right away.

Cooking

On the morning of the day you want to eat, preheat your sous vide water bath to 141°F / 60.5°C. Place the pouch in the water bath for 2 to 12 hours.

Finishing

Preheat a grill to high heat or a pan to medium-high heat.

Remove the chicken from the water bath and pat dry. Sprinkle the chicken with the remaining spice rub. Sear until just browned, about 1 or 2 minutes per side. Remove from the heat and serve.

MIXED HERB PESTO CHICKEN PASTA

Pre-Bath Time: 15 Minutes
Cooking Time: 2 to 12 Hours
Finishing Time: 30 Minutes
Temperature: 141°F / 60.5°C
Serves: 6

Pre-Bath Ingredients
For the Chicken
3-4 chicken breasts
1 tablespoon garlic powder
1 tablespoon onion powder
Pepper

Finishing Ingredients
For the Pesto
1½ cups fresh basil, packed
1 cup fresh parsley, packed
¼ cup pine nuts
½ teaspoon salt
¼ teaspoon black pepper
¼ cup fresh parmesan cheese
2 tablespoons lemon juice
4 cloves garlic, minced
½ cup olive oil

For the Pasta
1 pound fusilli pasta, or pasta of your choice
1 red pepper, cut into ¼" slices
Fresh parmesan cheese

Pesto is such a flavorful ingredient and it's very easy to make. Here we pair it with some pasta, chicken, and red pepper to make a filling dinner. You can also use it on a variety of meats or even as a rub before grilling.

Note: Usually chicken is best when cooked for 2 to 4 hours but during the week you can get away with cooking it for up to 12 hours with just a minimal loss in moisture.

Pre-Bath
Mix the spices together in a bowl. Pepper the chicken then sprinkle with the spice mixture and seal in a sous vide pouch.

At this point you can store the pouch in the refrigerator for up to 2 days, freeze it for up to 6 months, or cook it right away.

Cooking
On the morning of the day you want to eat, preheat your sous vide water bath to 141°F / 60.5°C. Place the pouch in the water bath for 2 to 12 hours.

Finishing
Preheat a grill to high heat or a pan to medium-high heat. Bring a pot of salted water to a boil.

Cook the fusilli until tender.

Make the pesto by combining all the ingredients into a blender or food processor and processing until it forms a smooth paste. This can be done a day or two ahead of time and stored in the refrigerator.

Remove the chicken from the water bath and pat dry. Sear until just browned, about 1 or 2 minutes per side. Remove from the heat and cut into ½" slices.

Place the cooked pasta into a bowl and combine with the pesto. Mix together well. Top with the red pepper and chicken. Grate some fresh parmesan cheese on top and serve.

BBQ Chicken Quesadillas

Pre-Bath Time: 15 Minutes
Cooking Time: 2 to 12 Hours
Finishing Time: 30 to 45 Minutes
Temperature: 141°F / 60.5°C
Serves: 4

Pre-Bath Ingredients
For the Chicken
2 chicken breasts
1 teaspoon garlic powder
½ teaspoon paprika
½ teaspoon ground cumin
½ teaspoon ground coriander
½ teaspoon ancho chile powder, or chile powder
  of your choice
Pepper

Finishing Ingredients
For the Quesadillas
8 flour tortillas
2 cups shredded Monterey Jack cheese
1 cup shredded cheddar cheese
1 sweet onion, thinly sliced
6 strips bacon, cooked and crumbled
BBQ Sauce, to taste

Canola or olive oil

BBQ chicken is one of my favorite ingredients in quesadillas or on pizza. We add Smoky bacon to it to pump the flavors up even more and give it some nice crunch. For even more flavor you can caramelize the onion before adding it to the quesadilla.

Note: Usually chicken is best when cooked for 2 to 4 hours but during the week you can get away with cooking it for up to 12 hours with just a minimal loss in moisture.

Pre-Bath
Mix the spices together in a bowl. Pepper the chicken then sprinkle with the spice mixture and seal in a sous vide pouch.

At this point you can store the pouch in the refrigerator for up to 2 days, freeze it for up to 6 months, or cook it right away.

Cooking
On the morning of the day you want to eat, preheat your sous vide water bath to 141°F / 60.5°C. Place the pouch in the water bath for 2 to 12 hours.

Finishing
Preheat a grill to high heat or a pan to medium-high heat.

Remove the chicken from the water bath and cut into ½" strips.

Lay out 4 of the tortillas and evenly split the chicken and other ingredients between them. Top each with a remaining tortilla.

Brush the top of each tortilla with oil and place it, oil side down, on the grill or in the pan. Cover the tortilla while it is cooking. Once it turns golden brown on the bottom flip it over and continue cooking until the cheese is melted and the quesadilla is browned on both sides.

Remove from the heat, cut into quarters, and serve.

CHICKEN TENDERS

Pre-Bath Time: 15 Minutes
Cooking Time: 2 to 12 Hours
Finishing Time: 40 Minutes
Temperature: 141°F / 60.5°C
Serves: 4

Pre-Bath Ingredients

For the Chicken
4 chicken breasts, cut into 1" strips
1 teaspoon garlic powder
1 teaspoon dried thyme
Pepper

Finishing Ingredients

For the Coating
¾ cup flour
2 teaspoons salt
1 teaspoon black pepper
2 eggs

For the Dipping Sauces
BBQ Sauce
Honey Mustard
Ranch Dressing

Chicken tenders are a great finger food that both kids and adults love. Since the chicken is cooked sous vide it remains nice and moist and you only have to focus on browning the coating when you finish cooking it. Serve it with a variety of dipping sauces so everyone can enjoy the combinations they prefer.

Note: Usually chicken is best when cooked for 2 to 4 hours but during the week you can get away with cooking it for up to 12 hours with just a minimal loss in moisture.

Pre-Bath

Pepper the chicken then sprinkle with the garlic and thyme. Place in the sous vide pouch and seal.

At this point you can store the pouch in the refrigerator for up to 2 days, freeze it for up to 6 months, or cook it right away.

Cooking

On the morning of the day you want to eat, preheat your sous vide water bath to 141°F / 60.5°C. Place the pouch in the water bath for 2 to 12 hours.

Finishing

Preheat a deep pan to medium-high heat.

First you will want to set up the stations for coating the chicken. Combine the flour, salt, and pepper on a plate. Beat the eggs into a wide mouth bowl.

Remove the chicken from the pouches and pat dry. Dredge the chicken in the flour, then the egg, then the flour once again.

Add about ½" of oil to the pan and sear the dredged chicken breasts until the crust becomes golden brown. Flip and cook the other side until browned. Remove from the heat and serve with the dipping sauces of your choice.

JAMAICAN JERK CHICKEN THIGHS

Pre-Bath Time: 30 Minutes
Cooking Time: 2 to 12 Hours
Finishing Time: 15 Minutes
Temperature: 148°F / 64.4°C
Serves: 4 to 6

Pre-Bath Ingredients
2-3 pounds of chicken thighs

For the Jerk Paste
3-10 habanero or Scotch bonnet chilies, to taste,
    stemmed and cut in half
1 onion, coarsely chopped
5 garlic cloves, coarsely chopped
½ cup chopped fresh parsley
½ cup chopped fresh cilantro
2 teaspoons fresh ginger, chopped
2 tablespoons fresh thyme
1 tablespoon ground allspice
½ teaspoon ground cinnamon
½ teaspoon freshly grated nutmeg
1 teaspoon freshly ground black pepper
¼ cup brown sugar
½ cup fresh lime juice
¼ cup olive oil
2 tablespoons soy sauce

Finishing Ingredients
None

Chicken thighs stand up great to this traditional Jamaican jerk flavoring but it can also be used on pork shoulder or chicken breast. A side of rice and beans or mashed plantains is a great complement to this dish.

To save even more time during the week you can find some good jerk pastes in the grocery store that will save you the time of preparing your own.

Note: Usually pork chops are best when cooked for 3 to 6 hours but during the week you can get away with cooking them for up to 12 hours with just a minimal loss in moisture.

Pre-Bath
First make the jerk paste. Add all of the dry ingredients to a food processor and process to a coarse paste. Add the remaining liquid ingredients and process until the paste becomes spreadable.

Smear the chicken thighs all over with the jerk paste. Add the thighs to the sous vide pouches and seal.

At this point you can store the pouch in the refrigerator for up to 2 days, freeze it for up to 6 months, or cook it right away.

Cooking
On the morning of the day you want to eat, preheat your sous vide water bath to 148°F / 64.4°C. Place the pouch in the water bath for 2 to 12 hours.

Finishing
Preheat a pan or grill to high heat.

Take the thighs out of the sous vide pouches and pat dry. Cook them at high heat for 1 to 2 minutes per side. Remove from the heat and serve.

CUBAN PORK CHOPS WITH MOJO SAUCE

Pre-Bath Time: 15 Minutes
Cooking Time: 3 to 12 Hours
Finishing Time: 30 Minutes
Temperature: 135°F / 57.5°C
Serves: 4

Pre-Bath Ingredients
For the Pork
4 pork chops
1 tablespoon garlic powder
1 bay leaf
Pepper

Finishing Ingredients
For the Mojo Sauce
3 tablespoons olive oil
8 cloves garlic, minced
⅓ cup orange juice
⅓ cup lime juice
1 teaspoon ground cumin
1 tablespoon chopped fresh oregano
Salt and pepper

Mojo sauce is a traditional cuban sauce often used for marinating pork. It often uses sour orange juice but we substitute ½ normal orange juice and ½ lime juice. We use the mojo as a mop as we grill the pork chops to add flavor to them.

Note: Usually pork chops are best when cooked for 3 to 6 hours but during the week you can get away with cooking them for up to 12 hours with just a minimal loss in moisture.

Pre-Bath
Lightly pepper the pork chops, sprinkle with the garlic powder, place in the sous vide pouch with the bay leaf and seal.

At this point you can store the pouch in the refrigerator for up to 2 days, freeze it for up to 6 months, or cook it right away.

Cooking
On the morning of the day you want to eat, preheat your sous vide water bath to 135°F / 57.2°C. Place the pouch in the water bath for 3 to 12 hours.

Finishing
Preheat a grill to high heat.

To prepare the mojo sauce heat the olive oil and garlic in a pan over medium-high heat. Cook until the garlic begins to soften, about 1 minute, then add the orange juice, lime juice and cumin. Bring to a simmer then stir in the oregano and remove from the heat.

Take the pork out of the pouches and pat dry. Sear them on the grill until grill marks form on the first side, a couple of minutes. Brush the mojo on the side facing up and flip the chops. Repeat several times until they are coated with the mojo, cooking about 30 to 45 seconds per turn.

Remove from the heat and serve with any excess mojo sauce on the side.

COCOA RUBBED PORK LOIN

Pre-Bath Time: 15 Minutes
Cooking Time: 4 to 12 Hours
Finishing Time: 15 Minutes
Temperature: 135°F / 57.5°C
Serves: 4

Pre-Bath Ingredients

For the Pork
2 pound pork loin roast
1 tablespoon ground coriander
1 teaspoon ground cinnamon
½ teaspoon nutmeg
½ teaspoon ground cloves
Pepper

Finishing Ingredients

For the Rub
2 tablespoons unsweetened cocoa
2 teaspoons ground cinnamon
½ teaspoon chipotle chile powder, or chile
   powder of your choice
Olive oil

*Most people think cocoa, cinnamon, and nutmeg can
only be used in desserts but they are actually great in
savory foods as well. Here we add them to a pork loin
roast for an unusual flavor that will have your family
wanting more.*

*Note: Usually pork loin roasts are best when cooked
for 4 to 8 hours but during the week you can get away
with cooking them for up to 12 hours with just a
minimal loss in moisture.*

Pre-Bath

Mix together the spices in a bowl. Lightly
pepper the pork loin roast and sprinkle with
the spices. Place in the sous vide pouch and
seal.

At this point you can store the pouch in the
refrigerator for up to 2 days, freeze it for up
to 6 months, or cook it right away.

Cooking

On the morning of the day you want to eat,
preheat your sous vide water bath to
135°F / 57.2°C. Place the pouch in the water
bath for 4 to 12 hours.

Finishing

Preheat a grill to high heat or a pan to
medium-high heat.

Combine the cocoa, cinnamon, and chile
powder in a bowl.

Take the pork out of the pouches and pat
dry. Lightly coat with cocoa spice mixture.
Drizzle with the oil to facilitate browning.
Sear the pork until it begins to brown, about
1 to 2 minutes per side.

Remove from the heat, slice into serving
portions, drizzle with more olive oil, and
serve.

ST. LOUIS STYLE RIBS

Pre-Bath Time: 15 Minutes
Cooking Time: 8 to 12 Hours
Finishing Time: 15 Minutes
Temperature: 135°F / 57.2°C
Serves: 2 to 4

Pre-Bath Ingredients

For the Ribs
2 pounds St. Louis style ribs, trimmed of excess
    fat and silverskin
1 tablespoon ground cumin
1 tablespoon garlic powder
2 dried bay leaves
1 tablespoon dried lemon peel (optional)
Pepper

Finishing Ingredients
½ cup your favorite BBQ sauce

Ribs are a great meal to cook during the week. After 10 to 12 hours in the water bath they become very tender and they are very quick to finish cooking. It's also very satisfying to dig into a big plate of them after a hard day of work.

I use St. Louis style ribs but baby back ribs will also work well. You can also cook them under the broiler if you don't want to grill them.

Pre-Bath
Mix together all the spices except the bay leaf in a bowl. Cut the ribs into pieces that will easily fit into your sous vide bags. Pepper the ribs and then coat them with the spice mix.

Place the ribs into the sous vide pouches, add the bay leaves, then seal. Be sure you don't seal the ribs too tightly or the bones may pierce the bag.

At this point you can store the pouch in the refrigerator for up to 2 days, freeze it for up to 6 months, or cook it right away.

Cooking
On the morning of the day you want to eat, preheat your sous vide water bath to 135°F / 57.2°C. Place the pouch in the water bath for 8 to 12 hours.

Finishing
Preheat a grill to high heat.

Remove the sous vide pouches from the water bath and take the ribs out of the pouches. Pat them dry and then coat with the BBQ sauce.

Quickly grill the ribs just until the BBQ sauce begins to caramelize, about 1 to 2 minutes per side. Take off the grill and serve.

MEMPHIS STYLE BABY BACK RIBS

Pre-Bath Time: 15 Minutes
Cooking Time: 8 to 12 Hours
Finishing Time: 15 Minutes
Temperature: 135°F / 57.2°C
Serves: 2 to 4

Pre-Bath Ingredients

For the Ribs
2 pounds baby back or back ribs, trimmed of
    excess fat and silverskin
2 tablespoons brown sugar
2 tablespoons paprika
1 tablespoon garlic powder
1 tablespoon ground black pepper
2 teaspoons onion powder
2 teaspoons dried thyme
1 teaspoon mustard powder
½ teaspoon chipotle chile powder or chile
    powder of your choice
½ teaspoon celery seeds

Finishing Ingredients
None

*These ribs use the typical Memphis style dry rub. I
like to add half the rub before cooking so the ribs
become infused with the flavor and then apply the
other half after sous viding so you get more of the
typical crust on the ribs.*

*Note: I use baby back ribs or back ribs but St. Louis
ribs will also work well.*

Pre-Bath

In a bowl mix together all the spices. Cut the
ribs into pieces that will easily fit into your
sous vide bags. Coat the ribs with half of the
spice mix.

Place the ribs into the sous vide pouches
then seal. Be sure you don't seal the ribs too
tightly or the bones may pierce the bag.

At this point you can store the pouch in the
refrigerator for up to 2 days, freeze it for up
to 6 months, or cook it right away.

Cooking

On the morning of the day you want to eat,
preheat your sous vide water bath to
135°F / 57.2°C. Place the pouch in the water
bath for 8 to 12 hours.

Finishing

Preheat a grill to high heat or a pan to
medium-high heat.

Remove the sous vide pouches from the
water bath and take the ribs out of the sous
vide pouches. Pat them dry and then
sprinkle the meaty side with the remaining
spice rub.

Quickly grill the ribs just until the meat is
seared, about 1 to 2 minutes per side. Take
off the grill and serve.

COUNTRY STYLE RIBS WITH SWEET APPLES

Pre-Bath Time: 10 Minutes
Cooking Time: 8 to 12 Hours
Finishing Time: 20 Minutes
Temperature: 135°F / 57.2°C
Serves: 2 to 4

Pre-Bath Ingredients
For the Ribs
4 pounds of country style ribs
2 tablespoons garlic powder
2 teaspoons cinnamon
1 teaspoon nutmeg
1 teaspoon ancho chile powder or chile powder
   of your choice
Pepper

Finishing Ingredients
3 tablespoons butter
3-4 red apples, cored and sliced
3 tablespoons brown sugar
1 ½ tablespoons lemon juice
2 tablespoons chopped mint

Pork and apples are a classic food pairing and here we achieve that with country style ribs with a sweet apple topping. The ribs are cooked for 8 to 12 hours until they are meltingly tender then the apples are cooked with butter and sugar until they begin to soften. Some mint and lemon juice pull the whole meal together.

Pre-Bath

In a bowl mix together all the spices. Cut the ribs into pieces that will easily fit into your sous vide bags. Pepper the ribs then coat with the spice mix.

Place the ribs into the sous vide pouches then seal. Be sure you don't seal the ribs too tightly or the bones may pierce the bag.

At this point you can store the pouch in the refrigerator for up to 2 days, freeze it for up to 6 months, or cook it right away.

Cooking
On the morning of the day you want to eat, preheat your sous vide water bath to 135°F / 57.2°C.

Place the pouch in the water bath for 8 to 12 hours.

Finishing
Preheat two pans to medium-high heat.

Melt the butter in one pan. Add the apples and cook until they turn tender. Sprinkle with the brown sugar and lemon juice and stir to combine. Remove from the heat and top with the chopped mint.

Remove the sous vide pouches from the water bath and take the ribs out of the sous vide pouches and pat them dry.

Add oil to the other pan and warm. Quickly cook the ribs just until the meat is seared, about 1 to 2 minutes per side. Take off the heat and serve topped with the apples.

MULTI-DAY MEATS

If you are interested in staying up to date with the work we are doing in sous vide feel free to follow us on Twitter. We post articles we find interesting, links to new recipes, and other items of interest.

We are @jasonlogsdon_sv

GENERAL PROCESS

Multi-Day Meats focus on foods that take an extended amount of time to cook, usually 1 to 3 days. The key to these recipes is to look at the cooking time and count back from when you want to eat. For example, if it's a 24 hour cook time you know to put it in the water bath around dinner time the day before.

Pre-Bath Stage

The *Pre-Bath* stage usually will consist of seasoning and bagging the food. Unless you need to cube or trim the meat it is a very quick process. You can do this prep work several days in advance if you are keeping it in the refrigerator or months in advance if you freeze the food once it's been bagged. You can also do it the day it goes into the water bath if that works best for you.

Cooking Stage

The *Cooking* stage will last for over 12 hours and up to several days. Be sure to look at the time the food needs to be in the water bath to determine when you should start it so it is ready when you will want to eat.

If the times don't match up for a dish you want to prepare you can always use the cook, chill, and hold method to store the meat for a longer period of time.

Finishing Stage

The *Finishing* stage will generally be completed right after you remove the food from the water bath. For most recipes you take the meat out of the pouch, pat it dry, and sear it. You also make any sides or salsas as well as make any side dishes or sauces for it.

COMMON MULTI-DAY MEATS

There are many cuts of meat that cook for several days. Here are some of the more popular ones.

Beef Roasts

Bottom Round Roast: 2-3 days
Chuck Roast: 2-3 days
Pot Roast: 2-3 days
Beef Ribs: 2-3 days
Beef Shank: 2-3 days
Short Ribs: 2-3 days
Top Round Roast: 1-3 days
Beef Cheek: 2-3 days
Brisket: 2-3 days

Beef Steaks

Bottom Round: 2-3 days
Chuck: 1-2 days
Eye Round: 1-2 days
Flank: 1-2 days
Skirt: 1-2 days
Top Round: 1-2 days

Lamb

Arm or Blade Chop: 18-36 hours
Breast: 20-28 hours
Leg, Bone In: 1-2 days
Leg, Boneless: 18-36 hours
Osso Buco or Shank: 1-2 days
Ribs: 22-26 hours
Shoulder: 1-2 days

Pork

Belly: 2-3 days
Boston Butt: 1-2 days
Butt Roast: 18-36 hours
Picnic Roast: 1-3 days
Shoulder: 1-2 days
Spare Ribs: 12-24 hours

Sweet and Savory Beef Roast

Pre-Bath Time: 20 Minutes
Cooking Time: 2 to 3 Days
Finishing Time: 15 Minutes
Temperature: 131°F / 55°C
Serves: 4 to 6

Pre-Bath Ingredients
2-3 pounds bottom round roast, trimmed of
  excess fat and silver skin

For the Rub
5 tablespoons brown sugar
3 tablespoons freshly ground black pepper
2 tablespoons dried thyme
1½ tablespoons onion powder
1½ tablespoons garlic powder
1 tablespoon ground coriander
½ teaspoon mustard powder
½ teaspoon cayenne pepper or chile powder of
  your choice
½ teaspoon celery seeds

Finishing Ingredients
None

*This sweet and savory rub works well on most kinds
of beef. It's also good on chicken and pork.*

*A great tasting and time saving tip is to make more
beef than you need for dinner and then chill the
extras. Once it's cold you can thinly slice it and use it
as lunch meat for the week. Or dice it and use it in
stir fries or chili.*

Pre-Bath
Mix together all the rub ingredients in a
bowl then coat the roast with it. Any extra
rub can be kept in a sealed container in a
cabinet for several months.

Add the roast to the sous vide pouch then
seal.

At this point you can store the pouch in the
refrigerator for up to 2 days, freeze it for up
to 6 months, or cook it right away.

Cooking
Preheat the water bath to 131°F / 55°C.

Place the pouch in the water bath for 2 to 3
days.

Finishing
Preheat a grill to high heat or a pan to
medium-high heat.

Take the beef out of the water bath and
remove it from the pouch. Pat it dry with a
paper towel or dish cloth. Quickly sear the
roast for 1 to 2 minutes per side, until just
browned, then remove from the heat.

Slice the roast, I prefer either very thin or ½"
thick, and serve. You can serve the juices
from the pouch on the side as au jus if you'd
like.

ACHIOTE BEEF WITH JALAPENO POLENTA

Pre-Bath Time: 15 Minutes
Cooking Time: 1 to 2 Days
Finishing Time: 30 Minutes
Temperature: 131°F / 55°C
Serves: 4 to 6

Pre-Bath Ingredients
For the Roast
2-3 pounds chuck roast
3 tablespoons achiote paste
Pepper

Finishing Ingredients
For the Polenta
2 tablespoons butter
2 jalapenos, diced
¼ cup milk
2 cups chicken stock
Water as per the directions on the polenta
   package
1 ⅓ cups quick cooking polenta
2 tablespoon chopped fresh cilantro
Salt and pepper

Achiote is a richly flavored paste from Central and South America made from annatto seeds mixed with other spices such as coriander, oregano, cumin, and garlic. You can find it on the international aisle of many grocery stores. We pair it with a creamy polenta with jalapenos in it but you could also use mashed potatoes if you prefer.

Pre-Bath
Coat the roast evenly with the achiote paste then pepper it. Add the roast to the sous vide pouch then seal.

At this point you can store the pouch in the refrigerator for up to 2 days, freeze it for up to 6 months, or cook it right away.

Cooking
Preheat the water bath to 131°F / 55°C.

Place the pouch in the water bath for 1 to 2 days.

Finishing
Preheat a grill to high heat or a pan to medium-high heat.

Heat a pot over medium-high heat. Add the butter and melt. Add the jalapeno and cook for a few minutes until it softens. Add the milk, chicken stock, and enough water to bring the volume of liquid to the amount called for by the directions on the polenta package. Bring the liquid to a boil and then whisk in the polenta and cook, stirring, until it thickens. Remove from the heat.

Take the beef out of the water bath and remove it from the pouch. Pat it dry with a paper towel or dish cloth. Quickly sear the roast for 1 to 2 minutes per side, until just browned, then remove from the heat.

Portion the beef and serve it on top of the polenta.

GARLIC CRUSTED TOP ROUND ROAST

Pre-Bath Time: 10 Minutes
Cooking Time: 1 to 3 Days
Finishing Time: 15 to 60 Minutes
Temperature: 131°F / 55°C
Serves: 4 to 6

Pre-Bath Ingredients

For the Roast
3-4 pounds top round roast
1 tablespoon garlic powder
1 tablespoon onion powder
1 tablespoon paprika powder
2 teaspoons mustard powder
1 teaspoon ancho chile powder or chile powder
    of your choice
4 thyme sprigs
4 rosemary sprigs
Pepper

Finishing Ingredients

For the Crust
8 garlic cloves, peeled
4 rosemary sprigs
4 thyme sprigs
2-4 tablespoons sweet marjoram
2-4 tablespoons olive oil

*I find top round roasts to be a little drier and less
flavorful than other roasts. However, they are usually
pretty inexpensive. Using sous vide helps to remedy
some of the dryness and applying a flavorful garlic
and herb crust helps to fix the blandness.*

*This is a big tasting meal that traditionally would
take hours in the kitchen to prepare. Using sous vide
you can reduce the actual work time to a few minutes.
Roasting the garlic takes longer than anything else
but it can be done a day or two ahead of time and
stored in the refrigerator.*

Pre-Bath

Mix the spices together in a bowl. Pepper
the roast then sprinkle with the spices. Place
in a pouch with the thyme and rosemary
then seal.

At this point you can store the pouch in the
refrigerator for up to 2 days, freeze it for up
to 6 months, or cook it right away.

Cooking

Preheat the water bath to 131°F / 55°C.

Place the pouch in the water bath for 1 to 3
days.

Finishing

40 to 60 minutes before the roast is done
wrap the garlic cloves in aluminum foil with
some olive oil and salt and place in a 400°F
oven or toaster oven for 30 to 45 minutes,
until soft. Remove and set aside to cool.

Preheat the broiler on the oven.

Right before the sous vide roast is done
make the paste for the crust. Combine all the
crust ingredients in a food processor and
process until it forms a thick paste.

Take the roast out of the water bath and
remove it from the pouch. Pat it dry with a
paper towel or dish cloth and place in a
roasting pan. Smear the sides and top of the
meat with the paste. Place the roast in the
oven until the crust begins to brown, about 5
minutes.

Slice the roast, I prefer either very thin or ½"
thick, and serve. You can also serve the
juices from the pouch as au jus.

FRENCH DIP SANDWICHES

Pre-Bath Time: 15 Minutes
Cooking Time: 1 to 3 Days
Finishing Time: 30 Minutes
Temperature: 131°F / 55°C
Serves: 4 to 6

Pre-Bath Ingredients

For the Sous Vide Roast
2 pounds top round roast
2 tablespoons butter

For the Spice Mixture
1 tablespoon garlic powder
2 teaspoons onion powder
1 teaspoon ancho chile powder or chile powder
   of your choice
1 teaspoon dried sage
½ teaspoon ground cloves
¼ teaspoon cinnamon
¼ teaspoon nutmeg
Pepper

Finishing Ingredients

4-6 hoagie rolls or small baguettes
8-12 slices swiss cheese

French dip sandwiches are a classic deli food and they are very easy to make at home using sous vide. Once the meat is cooked for several days it is seared and thinly sliced. I like to pile the slices on a hoagie roll with melted swiss cheese but you can serve it however you prefer. Many people enjoy thinly sliced red onion on it.

Pre-Bath

Mix together the spice ingredients in a bowl. Pepper the roast then cover with the spices. Place in a pouch with the butter then seal.

At this point you can store the pouch in the refrigerator for up to 2 days, freeze it for up to 6 months, or cook it right away.

Cooking

Preheat the water bath to 131°F / 55°C.

Place the pouch in the water bath for 1 to 3 days.

Finishing

Heat a pan over medium-high heat.

Remove the roast from the water bath, reserving the juice in the pouches, and pat dry. Quickly sear the roast in the pan until just browned, about 1 to 2 minutes per side. Remove from the heat and place on a cutting board.

Slice the meat as thinly as you can.

Place the cheese on the rolls and toast in an oven with the broiler on or toaster oven until the cheese melts and the buns begin to brown. Remove the rolls from the oven and pile the roast beef on top. Pour the reserved juices from the sous vide bag into ramekins or small bowls for dipping and serve.

CORNED BEEF REUBENS

Pre-Bath Time: 10 Minutes
Cooking Time: 1 to 3 Days
Finishing Time: 30 Minutes
Temperature: 135°F / 57°C
Serves: 4

Pre-Bath Ingredients
2-3 pounds cured, uncooked corned beef

Finishing Ingredients
8 slices rye bread
8 slices swiss cheese
About 1 cup thousand island dressing
High quality Dijon mustard
1 cup sauerkraut

Corned beef cooked with sous vide results in meat with great texture and tenderness. It is also juicier and more flavorful than many corned beefs.

In this recipe we call for it to be cooked at 135°F / 57°C which was the temperature we liked best. However, our test with the corned beef cooked at 146°F / 63.3°C was also very good. It was drier than the 135°F / 57°C meat but a bit more tender. Either temperature will result in fantastic corned beef.

Sometimes the corned beef will turn out too salty. If that is the case place it in a ziplock bag with some warm water and place back in the water bath. Over time the water in the bag will draw out the salt from the corned beef.

Pre-Bath
Place the corned beef in a sous vide pouch with any included spices then seal.

At this point you can store the pouch in the refrigerator for up to 2 days, freeze it for up to 6 months, or cook it right away.

Cooking
Preheat the water bath to 135°F / 57°C.

Place the pouch in the water bath for 1 to 3 days.

Finishing
Heat a pan over medium-high heat.

Remove the corned beef from the water bath and pat dry. Quickly sear it in the pan until just browned, about 1 to 2 minutes per side. Remove from the heat and slice into thin strips.

Brush one side of the bread slices with olive oil and toast until browned. Place the cheese on the un-toasted side of the bread and toast in a toaster oven or an oven with the broiler on until the cheese melts.

Add the thousand island dressing to four of the slices and the mustard to the other four. Pile the corned beef on the slices with mustard and top with the sauerkraut. Place the two halves together and serve.

Smoky BBQ Beef Ribs

Pre-Bath Time: 15 Minutes
Cooking Time: 2 to 3 Days
Finishing Time: 30 Minutes
Temperature: 131°F / 55°C
Serves: 4 to 8

Pre-Bath Ingredients
For the Ribs
3-4 pounds beef ribs
2 tablespoons paprika
1 tablespoon onion powder
½ tablespoon coriander
½ tablespoon chipotle chile powder or chile
   powder of your choice
1-2 tablespoons liquid smoke
Pepper

Finishing Ingredients
For the Salsa
1 avocado, diced
1 cup diced pineapple
½ cup corn kernels, cooked
1 tablespoon lime juice
2 tablespoons olive oil
3 tablespoons chopped fresh cilantro

These ribs are very easy to make and come out very flavorful and tender. For even more flavor you can serve them with your favorite BBQ sauce. The salsa is an easy way to add flavors to the meal while still letting the ribs shine.

Pre-Bath
Combine the spice ingredients in a bowl. Pepper the beef ribs then sprinkle with the spice mixture. Add to the sous vide pouches along with the liquid smoke and seal.

At this point you can store the pouch in the refrigerator for up to 2 days, freeze it for up to 6 months, or cook it right away.

Cooking
Preheat the water bath to 131°F / 55°C.

Place the pouch in the water bath for 2 to 3 days.

Finishing
Preheat a grill to high heat or a pan to medium-high heat.

Mix together all of the salsa ingredients in a bowl and set aside.

Take the ribs out of the water bath and remove them from the pouches. Pat them dry with a paper towel or dish cloth. Quickly sear the ribs on the grill or pan for about 1 to 2 minutes per side, until just browned. Remove from the heat and serve with a spoonful or two of the salsa.

SMOKY BEEF BRISKET

Pre-Bath Time: 15 Minutes
Cooking Time: 1 to 3 Days
Finishing Time: 15 Minutes
Temperature: 135°F / 57.2°C
Serves: 4 to 8

Pre-Bath Ingredients
3-4 pound brisket
1 tablespoon liquid smoke

For the Rub
2 tablespoons paprika
2 tablespoons garlic powder
2 tablespoons ground cumin
2 tablespoons ground coriander
1 teaspoon cinnamon
1 teaspoon dried oregano
1 teaspoon chipotle powder

Finishing Ingredients
None

During the week it's hard to find time to smoke foods. Using liquid smoke during the cooking helps to impart the Smoky flavor without requiring all the hard work. I often serve this brisket with corn bread and macaroni and cheese. You can also add your favorite BBQ sauce to it at the end for even more flavor.

Pre-Bath
Mix together all the rub ingredients in a bowl. Pepper the brisket then coat with the spices. Place in a sous vide pouch with the liquid smoke then seal.

At this point you can store the pouch in the refrigerator for up to 2 days, freeze it for up to 6 months, or cook it right away.

Cooking
Preheat the water bath to 135°F / 57.2°C.

Place the pouch in the water bath for 1 to 3 days.

Finishing
Preheat a grill to high heat or a pan to medium-high heat.

Take the brisket out of the water bath and remove it from the pouch. Pat it dry with a paper towel or dish cloth. Quickly sear the brisket for about 1 to 2 minutes per side, just until browned.

Take the brisket off the heat, slice ⅛" to ¼" thick, and serve.

BEEF CHILI

Pre-Bath Time: 15 Minutes
Cooking Time: 12 to 48 Hours
Finishing Time: 30 Minutes
Temperature: 131°F / 55°C
Serves: 8

Pre-Bath Ingredients
For the Meat
2 pounds stew meat or chuck roast cut into ½" chunks
1 tablespoon garlic powder
1 tablespoon ancho powder, or chile powder of your choice
1 teaspoon chipotle powder, or chile powder of your choice
1 teaspoon ground cumin
Pepper

Finishing Ingredients
For the Chile Base
1 onion, diced
1 red pepper, diced
4 cloves garlic, diced
2 teaspoons paprika
2 bay leaves
28 ounces diced tomatoes, canned
28 ounces crushed tomatoes, canned
½ cup tomato paste
1 can black beans
1 cup chicken stock
Salt and pepper

For the Garnish
2 tablespoons chopped fresh cilantro
¼ cup shredded cheddar cheese
Sour cream

This recipe has a wide range of cook times because it really depends on the type of stew meat used and how tender you want it. Some people prefer their chili meat very tender but I prefer it cooked for a shorter time so it has more bite to it. You can get the specific time by looking at the table in the back of the book once you purchase your meat.

Pre-Bath
Mix the spices together in a bowl. Season the meat with pepper, then sprinkle with the spices. Place in a sous vide pouch and seal.

At this point you can store the pouch in the refrigerator for up to 2 days, freeze it for up to 6 months, or cook it right away.

Cooking
Preheat the water bath to 131°F / 55°C.

Place the pouches in the water bath and cook for 12 to 48 hours.

Finishing
Heat up some oil in a deep frying pan or pot over medium-high heat.

Add the onion to the pan and cook for several minutes, until it begins to become translucent. Add the red pepper and saute for another 2 minutes.

Add the remaining ingredients to the pan and mix well. Cook until the chili comes together and begins to thicken, about 10 to 15 minutes. At this point you can let it simmer for up to an hour to intensify the flavor and thicken it.

Remove the beef from the sous vide pouches and add to the chile, along with the liquid in the pouches, and mix well. Ladle the chile into bowls and add the chopped cilantro and shredded cheese. Top with a dollop of sour cream and serve.

SHORT RIBS WITH ASIAN CITRUS SAUCE

Pre-Bath Time: 15 Minutes
Cooking Time: 2 to 3 Days
Finishing Time: 20 Minutes
Temperature: 135°F / 57°C
Serves: 4

Pre-Bath Ingredients

For the Ribs
3-4 pounds of short ribs, trimmed of excess silver
    skin and fat
4 tablespoons Chinese 5-spice powder
2 thyme sprigs
Pepper

Finishing Ingredients

For the Sauce
1 tablespoon rice wine vinegar
2 tablespoons orange juice
1 tablespoon peanut oil or olive oil
2 tablespoons oyster sauce
1 tablespoon brown sugar
½ teaspoon chipotle chile powder, or chile
    powder of your choice

For the Garnish
2 tablespoons orange zest
2 scallions, sliced

*This is an Asian take on traditional short ribs. We
season the ribs with Chinese 5-spice powder before
sous viding them and then make a simple sauce to
pour over them. I usually serve these with some white
rice to soak up the sauce.*

Pre-Bath

Pepper the ribs and sprinkle with the
Chinese 5-spice powder. Place in a sous vide
pouch with the thyme and seal.

At this point you can store the pouch in the
refrigerator for up to 2 days, freeze it for up
to 6 months, or cook it right away.

Cooking

Preheat your sous vide water bath to 135°F /
57°C.

Place the pouch in the water bath for 2 to 3
days.

Finishing

Preheat a grill to high heat or the broiler on
your oven.

Whisk together all the ingredients for the
sauce until thoroughly combined.

Remove the short ribs from the sous vide
pouches and pat them dry with a paper
towel or dish cloth. Quickly sear the ribs for
about 1 to 2 minutes per side, until just
browned. Brush the sauce over the ribs and
sear for 30 seconds. Brush the other side
with the sauce and sear for another 30
seconds.

Place the ribs on individual plates, spoon
the sauce over them, sprinkle with the
scallions and orange zest, then serve.

CUBAN SPICED CHUCK STEAK

Pre-Bath Time: 10 Minutes
Cooking Time: 1 to 3 Days
Finishing Time: 30 Minutes
Temperature: 131°F / 55°C
Serves: 4

Pre-Bath Ingredients
For the Roast
2 pounds chuck roast or steak, cut into 1"-1½"
   thick serving portions
1 tablespoon garlic powder
2 teaspoons ground cumin
1 teaspoon dried oregano
1 bay leaf
Pepper

Finishing Ingredients
For the Salsa
3 tomatillos, diced
2 medium tomatoes, diced
½ red onion, diced
1 red pepper, diced
2 tablespoons chopped fresh oregano
1 tablespoon orange juice
1 tablespoon lime juice
2 tablespoons olive oil
Salt and pepper

Chuck is one of my favorite cuts of beef to cook sous vide. It's a relatively tough cut but one that is full of flavor and sous vide renders it as tender as filet. It's also a great way to save money since it's normally about one third the cost of "better" cuts of steak.

Pre-Bath
Mix the spices together in a bowl. Pepper the chuck steak then sprinkle the with spices. Place it into the sous vide pouch with the bay leaf and seal.

At this point you can store the pouch in the refrigerator for up to 2 days, freeze it for up to 6 months, or cook it right away.

Cooking
Preheat the water bath to 131°F / 55°C.

Place the pouch in the water bath for 1 to 3 days.

Finishing
Preheat a grill to high heat or a pan to medium-high heat.

Make the salsa by combining all the ingredients in a bowl. Salt and pepper to taste.

Take the steaks out of the pouches and pat dry. Sear the steaks until just browned, 1 to 2 minutes per side. Remove from the heat and serve with a scoop or two of the salsa on top.

Perfect Pot Roast with Root Vegetables

Pre-Bath Time: 15 Minutes
Cooking Time: 2 to 3 Days
Finishing Time: 45 Minutes
Temperature: 135°F / 57.2°C
Serves: 4 to 8

Pre-Bath Ingredients

For the Roast
3 pounds pot roast, trimmed of excess fat and
　　silver skin
1 tablespoon garlic powder
1 tablespoon paprika
3 rosemary sprigs
3 thyme sprigs
Pepper

Finishing Ingredients

For the Vegetables
2 tablespoons canola oil
1 yellow onion, coarsely diced
2 cloves garlic, diced
4 large carrots, peeled and cut into ½" rounds
2 red potatoes, diced
3 tablespoons butter
1 pint baby bella or white button mushrooms,
　　quartered
Salt and pepper

For the Gravy
1 cup beef or chicken stock
2 tablespoons flour
2 tablespoons cold water
4 tablespoons of butter, cut into slices

Pot roasts are a classic comfort food but we've all had ones that come out dry and bland. Using sous vide to cook it ensures that is will stay moist while tenderizing. It comes out more like a good steak than a traditional pot roast.

To save time you can also cut the vegetables a day or two ahead of time and store them in the refrigerator. Then on the day of cooking you can just add them to the pan directly.

Pre-Bath

Pepper the roast then sprinkle with the garlic and paprika. Place in the sous vide pouch with the rosemary and thyme then seal.

At this point you can store the pouch in the refrigerator for up to 2 days, freeze it for up to 6 months, or cook it right away.

Cooking

Preheat the water bath to 135°F / 57.2°C. Place the pouch in the water bath for 2 to 3 days.

Finishing

Preheat a pot to medium-high heat.

In the pot add the onion and cook until it begins to soften, 3 to 4 minutes. Add the garlic, carrots, and potatoes and cook until tender, another 10 to 15 minutes. Remove them from the pot and add the butter to the pot. Once it is melted, add the mushrooms and cook until tender 5 to 10 minutes. Remove the mushrooms from the pot.

Preheat another pan to medium-high heat.

Take the roast out of the water bath and remove it from the pouch, reserving the liquid. Pat it dry with a paper towel or dish cloth.

Place the reserved liquid into the pot, add the stock and bring to a boil. Mix together the flour and cold water in a bowl then whisk into the pot. Bring to a boil then reduce the heat to medium-low.

Quickly sear the roast in the pan for 1 to 2 minutes per side, until just browned.

While the meat is cooking stir the butter into the gravy one tablespoon at a time.

Take the pot roast off the heat, thickly slice it, and serve with the vegetables and a spoonful or two of gravy on top.

ARGENTINIAN FLANK STEAK WITH CHIMICHURRI

Pre-Bath Time: 10 Minutes
Cooking Time: 2 to 12 Hours or 1 to 2 Days
Finishing Time: 20 Minutes
Temperature: 131°F / 55°C
Serves: 4 to 6

Pre-Bath Ingredients
For the Steak
2-4 pounds flank steak
2 tablespoons garlic powder
2 tablespoons cumin powder
2 tablespoons ancho chile powder, or chile
    powder of your choice
Pepper

Finishing Ingredients
For the Chimichurri
1 bunch culantro or cilantro
6 garlic cloves, coarsely chopped
3 tablespoons onion, diced
5 tablespoons cider vinegar
4 tablespoons water
2 teaspoons dried oregano
1 teaspoon hot pepper flakes, or to taste
Salt and pepper
1 cup olive oil

Chimichurri is usually made with culantro, but that can be very hard to find so here I substitute cilantro, which has a similar flavor. You can also use parsley if you prefer. I like serving this with a yellow or white rice or roasted potatoes.

Note: I prefer my flank steak to have some bite to it so I normally cook it for 2 to 12 hours but some people prefer it to be meltingly tender and cook it for 1 to 2 days. If you want to try that then start it in the water bath 1 to 2 days before you want to eat.

Pre-Bath
Mix together the spices in a bowl. Pepper the steak then sprinkle with the spice mixture. Add to the sous vide pouch and seal.

At this point you can store the pouch in the refrigerator for up to 2 days, freeze it for up to 6 months, or cook it right away.

Cooking
Preheat the water bath to 131°F / 55°C.

Place the pouch in the water bath for 2 to 12 Hours or 1 to 2 days.

Finishing
Preheat a grill to high heat or a pan to medium-high heat.

To make the chimichurri, put the cilantro and garlic in a food processor and process until finely chopped. Add the rest of the ingredients, except for the olive oil, and process until lightly mixed. Add the oil in a thin stream while processing until the sauce comes together.

Take the steaks out of the pouches and pat dry. Sear until just browned, about 1 to 2 minutes per side. Cut the steak into ⅛" to ¼" strips and place on a plate. Top with a spoonful or two of the chimichurri.

LAMB CURRY

Pre-Bath Time: 15 Minutes
Cooking Time: 2 to 3 Days
Finishing Time: 45 Minutes
Cooking Time: 2 to 3 Days
Temperature: 131°F / 55°C
Serves: 4

Pre-Bath Ingredients
For the Lamb
2 pounds boneless leg of lamb, cut into 1"-2"
   chunks
2 teaspoons garam masala
Pepper

Finishing Ingredients
For the Curry
3 onions, chopped
5 garlic cloves, coarsely chopped
2-inch piece fresh ginger, peeled and cut into
   large chunks
3 tablespoons canola oil
2 carrots, peeled and chopped
1 red bell pepper, chopped
2 teaspoons ground coriander
½ teaspoon black pepper
½ teaspoon ground cloves
¼-1 teaspoon cayenne pepper, to taste
½ teaspoon garam masala
½ cup plain yogurt, preferable whole milk
1½ cups water
¼ cup heavy cream
¼ cup fresh parsley, chopped
Salt and pepper

*This is a classic curry featuring boneless leg of lamb.
It can also be used with chicken or pork. Serve it with
rice and bread to soak up sauce and maybe a crisp
salad to offset the richness of the curry.*

Pre-Bath

Pepper the lamb then sprinkle with the
garam masala. Place into the sous vide
pouch and seal.

At this point you can store the pouch in the
refrigerator for up to 2 days, freeze it for up
to 6 months, or cook it right away.

Cooking

Preheat the water bath to 131°F / 55°C.

Place the pouch in the water bath for 2 to 3
days.

Finishing

About 30 to 45 minutes before the lamb is
done start working on the curry.

Add half the onion and all of the garlic and
ginger to a food processor. Process to a
paste.

Warm a pan over medium-high heat with
the canola oil in it. Add the remaining onion
and cook until it begins to soften, about 5
minutes. Add the carrots and cook for
another 5 minutes. Add the red bell pepper
and cook for another 5 minutes.

Add the pureed onion mixture, the
coriander, pepper, cayenne, garam masala,
and cloves to the pan. Cook for about 10
minutes while stirring occasionally.

Add the yogurt and water and bring to a
simmer. Remove the lamb from the sous
vide pouches and add to the pan, along with
some of the juices from the pouch. Stir well
and let simmer for about 5 minutes.

Stir in the cream and parsley and serve,
preferably over rice or with crusty bread.

BROWN SUGAR GLAZED LEG OF LAMB

Pre-Bath Time: 15 Minutes
Cooking Time: 2 to 3 Days
Finishing Time: 20 Minutes
Temperature: 131°F / 55°C
Serves: 4

Pre-Bath Ingredients
For the Lamb
2 pounds boneless leg of lamb
1 tablespoon garlic powder
1 tablespoon onion powder
2 thyme sprigs
2 rosemary sprigs
Pepper

Finishing Ingredients
For the Glaze
½ cup firmly packed brown sugar
2 tablespoons prepared mustard
2 tablespoons cider vinegar
2 tablespoons orange juice

Leg of lamb can benefit a lot from sous vide, coming out nice and tender while still being medium rare. Here we add a glaze at the end to wrap it with additional flavor. The glaze also works great with pork.

Pre-Bath

Mix together the spices in a bowl. Pepper the lamb then sprinkle with the spices. Place into a sous vide pouch with the thyme and rosemary and seal.

At this point you can store the pouch in the refrigerator for up to 2 days, freeze it for up to 6 months, or cook it right away.

Cooking

Preheat the water bath to 131°F / 55°C.

Place the pouch in the water bath for 2 to 3 days.

Finishing

Preheat a grill to high heat or the broiler on your oven.

Make the glaze by combining all the ingredients in a bowl and mixing well.

Remove the lamb from the water bath and pat dry. Sear over high heat until browned, 1 to 2 minutes per side. Brush with the glaze and cook for another minute per side. Add the glaze once or twice more while searing. Remove from the heat, slice the lamb into portions and serve with some glaze drizzled on top.

MINTY LAMB SHANK WITH ROASTED TOMATOES

Pre-Bath Time: 10 Minutes
Cooking Time: 1 to 2 Days
Finishing Time: 30 Minutes
Temperature: 131°F / 55°C
Serves: 4

Pre-Bath Ingredients
For the Lamb
4 lamb shanks, about 3-4 pounds total
3 thyme sprigs
3 rosemary sprigs
Pepper

Finishing Ingredients
For the Tomatoes
1 pint cherry tomatoes
2 tablespoons chopped fresh rosemary
2 tablespoons fresh thyme leaves
2 tablespoons olive oil
Salt and pepper

For the Dressing
1 cup unflavored, whole yogurt
½ cup finely chopped mint leaves
1½ tablespoons lemon juice
Salt and pepper

Cooking lamb shank sous vide at a low temperature results in a much different taste and texture than traditional braised or roasted shank does. Here we pair it with a minty dressing and roasted tomatoes to complement it.

Pre-Bath
Season the lamb with pepper and place into a sous vide pouch. Add the thyme and rosemary and seal.

At this point you can store the pouch in the refrigerator for up to 2 days, freeze it for up to 6 months, or cook it right away.

Cooking
Preheat the water bath to 131°F / 55°C.

Place the pouch in the water bath for 1 to 2 days.

Finishing
Preheat a pan to medium-high heat. Preheat the oven to 400°F / 204°C.

Toss the tomatoes with the herbs and olive oil then salt and pepper them. Place on a baking sheet with raised edges and bake until the tomatoes burst, 5 to 15 minutes.

Make the dressing by combining all of the ingredients in a bowl and mixing well.

Take the lamb out of the sous vide pouches and pat dry. Sear the lamb just until browned, about 1 to 2 minutes per side. Remove the lamb from the heat and place on individual plates.

Drizzle the lamb with the dressing and top with the roasted tomatoes.

PULLED PORK WITH BOURBON BBQ SAUCE

Pre-Bath Time: 15 Minutes
Cooking Time: 1 to 2 Days
Finishing Time: 30 Minutes
Temperature: 135°F / 57.2°C
Serves: 5 to 10

Pre-Bath Ingredients
For the Pork
4-5 pounds pork shoulder, trimmed of excess fat
1 tablespoon ancho chile powder or chile
    powder of your choice
1 tablespoon cumin
1 tablespoon coriander
1 tablespoon liquid smoke
1 tablespoon Worcester sauce
Pepper

Finishing Ingredients
For the BBQ Sauce
2 cups ketchup
1 cup Bourbon whiskey
½ cup brown sugar
½ cup water
¼ cup balsamic vinegar
3 tablespoons chopped garlic
1 tablespoon ancho chile powder or chile
    powder of your choice
2 tablespoons liquid smoke
2 tablespoons Worcester sauce
½ tablespoon chipotle chile powder or chile
    powder of your choice
1 tablespoon molasses
2 tablespoons whole grain mustard

Pulled pork is very easy to make with sous vide. We pair it with a very simple BBQ sauce but you can save time by using your favorite store brand or by making extra sauce to store in the refrigerator or freezer.

You can use extra pork in sandwiches, tacos, on nachos, or freeze it in 1 cup portions for later use.

Pre-Bath
Mix the spices together in a bowl. Pepper the pork shoulder, then coat with the spices. Place it in the pouch with the Worcester sauce and liquid smoke. Seal the pouch.

At this point you can store the pouch in the refrigerator for up to 2 days, freeze it for up to 6 months, or cook it right away.

Cooking
Preheat the water bath to 135°F / 57.2°C.

Place the pouch in the water bath for 1 to 2 days.

Finishing
Preheat a grill to high heat or a pan to medium-high heat.

When you're getting close to serving the pork you will want to make the BBQ sauce. Whisk together all of the ingredients in a pot over medium-high heat and bring to a simmer. Gently simmer for 5 to 10 minutes and then remove from the heat.

Remove the pork from the sous vide pouch and pat dry. Quickly sear the pork on all sides, 1 or 2 minutes per side, until just browned. Remove from the heat and chop into small pieces.

Serve with a spoonful of the BBQ sauce over top.

TERIYAKI SPARE RIBS

Pre-Bath Time: 10 Minutes
Cooking Time: 12 to 24 Hours
Finishing Time: 25 Minutes
Temperature: 135°F / 57.2°C
Serves: 2 to 4

Pre-Bath Ingredients
For the Ribs
2-3 pounds of pork spare ribs
2 tablespoons Chinese 5-spice powder
1 tablespoon ginger powder
Pepper

Finishing Ingredients
For the Teriyaki Sauce
⅓ cup soy sauce
¼ cup hoisin sauce
¼ cup brown sugar
½ cup diced pineapple
1 fresh red chile, diced
2 garlic cloves, diced
1 tablespoon grated ginger
3 tablespoons rice vinegar

Teriyaki is one of my favorite sauces. Much like BBQ sauce there are so many variations of it and no "right" one. Here is one that I enjoy that is also easy to put together. To save time you can always use a bottle of your favorite teriyaki sauce or make extra sauce and save it in the refrigerator or freezer for later use.

Pre-Bath
Cut the ribs into pieces that will easily fit into your sous vide bags. Pepper them then sprinkle with the Chinese 5-spice powder and the ginger. Place the ribs into the sous vide pouches and seal. Be sure you don't seal the ribs too tightly or the bones may pierce the bag.

At this point you can store the pouch in the refrigerator for up to 2 days, freeze it for up to 6 months, or cook it right away.

Cooking
Preheat the water bath to 135°F / 57.2°C.

Place the pouch in the water bath for 12 to 24 hours.

Finishing
Preheat a pan and a pot over medium-high heat.

In the pot combine all of the teriyaki sauce ingredients and bring to a simmer. Gently simmer for 5 minutes and remove from the heat.

Take the ribs out of the sous vide pouches and pat them dry. Sear the ribs until just browned, about 1 to 2 minutes per side. Take off the heat and serve with the teriyaki sauce on top.

PORK CARNITAS

Pre-Bath Time: 15 Minutes
Cooking Time: 1 to 3 Days
Finishing Time: 30 Minutes
Temperature: 135°F / 57.2°C
Serves: 4 to 6

Pre-Bath Ingredients

For the Sous Vide Roast
2 pounds pork butt or picnic roast, sliced into 2"
    slabs
2 tablespoons garlic powder
1 tablespoon onion powder
1 tablespoon paprika powder
1 teaspoon ancho chile powder or chile powder
    of your choice
½ teaspoon chipotle chile powder or chile
    powder of your choice
½ teaspoon dried oregano
5 sprigs fresh thyme
1 teaspoon liquid smoke
3 tablespoons lard or butter
Pepper

Finishing Ingredients

Garnishes for the Carnitas
Warm corn tortillas
1 lime, cut into eighths
Shredded lettuce
Guacamole
Sour cream
Queso fresco or feta cheese

*Pork carnitas are a very tender and moist Mexican
dish. Traditionally you slow cook the pork butt in lard
and then shred it. Here we cook it with sous vide
which eliminates a lot of the lard and also removes
some of the cooking steps.*

*This meat is also fantastic in burritos, on nachos, in
tacos, or on pizza. Often times I'll double this recipe
and use the leftovers throughout the week or freeze
them in 1 cup portions for later use.*

Pre-Bath

Mix together the spice ingredients in a bowl.
Pepper the roast then sprinkle with the
spices. Place in a pouch with the thyme,
liquid smoke, and butter then seal.

At this point you can store the pouch in the
refrigerator for up to 2 days, freeze it for up
to 6 months, or cook it right away.

Cooking

Preheat the water bath to 135°F / 57.2°C.

Place the pouch in the water bath for 1 to 3
days.

Finishing

Preheat a grill to high heat or a pan to
medium-high heat.

Remove the pork from the sous vide pouch,
reserving the juices, and pat dry. Quickly
sear the pork on all sides, about 1 or 2
minutes per side until just browned.
Remove from the heat.

Roughly chop the pork and place into a
bowl. Add some of the juices from the sous
vide pouch until it is moist but not soupy.

Serve the chopped pork with the warm corn
tortillas and other garnishes.

FAST COOKERS

If you are interested in staying up to date with sous vide you can join our free newsletter and get monthly sous vide tips and links to the best articles on the internet.

You can join our newsletter here:
http://bit.ly/ey9R5C

GENERAL PROCESS

Fast Cookers are foods that can be cooked in a shorter amount of time. Because of this, you can put them in right before you want to eat. Things like fish, chicken, and tender beef all fall into this category.

Pre-Bath Stage

The *Pre-Bath* stage usually will consist of seasoning and bagging the food. Unless you need to cube or trim the meat it is a very quick process. You can do this prep work several days in advance if you are keeping it in the refrigerator or months in advance if you freeze the food once it's been bagged. You can also do it the day it goes into the water bath if that works best for you.

Often times, I'll pre-package the food so I can put it into the bath as soon as I get home. That way I still have an hour or so to get changed, make the sides, and relax for a bit before the food is ready.

Cooking Stage

The *Cooking* stage will last for a relatively short amount of time ranging from 15 to 30 minutes for fish to 60 to 120 minutes for chicken and beef. For fish the cooking time can be pre-set but for chicken and beef you will need to reference the "Cooking By Thickness" section since the time will be based on the thickness of your food.

You can also hold these meals to eat at a later time using the cook, chill, and hold technique, though it usually doesn't save you much time for fish.

Finishing Stage

The *Finishing* stage will generally be completed right after you remove the food from the water bath. For most recipes you take the meat out of the pouch, pat it dry, and sear it. You also make any sides or salsas for it.

COMMON FAST COOKERS

Here are some of the more common foods you can cook in under 2 hours.

Beef

Tender cuts of beef are great for fast cooking. I often use ribeye, filet mignon or tenderloin, porterhouse, loin strip, and hanger steaks.

Fish

Almost any kind of fish or shellfish can be cooked in a short amount of time.

Pork

Smaller cuts of pork such as chops or portioned loin can be cooked quickly.

Poultry

Chicken and turkey breasts, thighs, and legs can all be cooked quickly, but thighs and breasts are fastest since you can make them thinner by butterflying them or cutting them in half width-wise.

TIPS AND TRICKS

Make Meat Thinner

The amount of time it takes to cook beef, pork, and poultry is directly related to the thickness of the meat. For instance, it takes a ½" (13 mm) steak about 12 minutes to heat up but a 1½" (38mm) steak takes almost 2 hours. So if you want to eat faster when you get home cook thinner cuts and save the juicy cuts for the weekend when you have more time.

This also works for chicken. If you butterfly a chicken breast, or just cut in half width-wise, you can knock 30 to 60 minutes off your cooking time.

Add Directly From the Freezer

Heating food directly from the freezer doesn't take significantly longer than if it's been in the refrigerator. Frozen food takes about an extra 20% of the time that refrigerated food does. That means a typical steak or piece of fish (around ½ to 1 inch thick) will only take an extra 2 to 10 minutes to cook if it was frozen.

Prep Ahead of Time

If I really want to get the food on the table quickly after I get home I make sure I already have the food prepped and bagged. That way it's all ready to go in the bath and I can start on the sides and sauces right away.

PEPPERED FILET MIGNON WITH BLUE CHEESE

Pre-Bath Time: 15 Minutes
Cooking Time: See "Cooking by Thickness"
Finishing Time: 15 Minutes
Temperature: 131°F / 55°C
Serves: 4

Pre-Bath Ingredients
For the Steak
4 portions of filet mignon, preferably 1" or less
    thick
2 thyme sprigs
1 rosemary sprig
Pepper

Finishing Ingredients
½ cup crumbled blue cheese
Fresh coarsely ground black pepper
Salt

This is a quick and easy way to have a classic steak house meal. The cheese adds a nice richness to the steak without overwhelming the flavor of the meat and the peppercorns give it a nice peppery finish. It's great when served with thick steak fries or a loaded baked potato.

Pre-Bath
Pepper the meat then place in the sous vide pouch with the thyme and rosemary. Seal the pouch.

At this point you can store the pouch in the refrigerator for up to 2 days, freeze it for up to 6 months or cook it right away.

Cooking
Preheat the water bath to 131°F / 55°C.

Place the sous vide pouch in the water bath and cook for the amount of time indicated in the "Cooking by Thickness" section for the time for heating beef from the refrigerator or freezer.

Finishing
Preheat a pan to medium-high heat or a grill to high heat. Preheat the broiler on your oven.

Take the steaks out of the pouches and pat dry. Grind the pepper on top and sear until browned, about 1 to 2 minutes per side. Remove from the heat and place on a roasting sheet.

Cover with the blue cheese. Place under the broiler and cook until the cheese begins to bubble. Remove from the heat and serve.

Ribeye with Spicy Sweet Mint Glaze

Pre-Bath Time: 10 Minutes
Cooking Time: See "Cooking by Thickness"
Finishing Time: 15 Minutes
Temperature: 131°F / 55°C
Serves: 2

Pre-Bath Ingredients

For the Steak
1-1½ pounds ribeye steak
1 teaspoon paprika
½ teaspoon chipotle chile powder or chile
   powder of your choice
Pepper

Finishing Ingredients

For the Glaze
4 tablespoons mustard, preferably Dijon
1¼ tablespoons bottled horseradish
1½ tablespoons chopped mint leaves
3 tablespoons honey
Salt and pepper

Ribeye is a very rich, flavorful cut of meat and it holds up will to the sweet mint glaze we use here. The mustard helps hold the glaze together as well as giving it a great taste.

Pre-Bath

Pepper the steak the sprinkle with the paprika and chile powder. Place in the sous vide pouch and seal.

At this point you can store the pouch in the refrigerator for up to 2 days, freeze it for up to 6 months or cook it right away.

Cooking

Preheat the water bath to 131°F / 55°C.

Place the sous vide pouch in the water bath and cook for the amount of time indicated in the "Cooking by Thickness" section for the time for heating beef from the refrigerator or freezer.

Finishing

Preheat a grill to high heat or the broiler on your oven.

Whisk together all the glaze ingredients in a small bowl and set aside. Remove the steaks from the sous vide pouches and pat dry. Coat the steaks with the glaze and cook for 1 to 2 minutes per side, brushing on more glaze when you turn them. Repeat this once or twice, being sure not to overcook the steaks. Remove from the heat and serve.

PORTERHOUSE WITH PICO DE GALLO

Pre-Bath Time: 15 Minutes
Cooking Time: See "Cooking by Thickness"
Finishing Time: 25 Minutes
Temperature: 131°F / 55°C
Serves: 4

Pre-Bath Ingredients

For the Steak
2 porterhouse steaks, preferably 1" or less thick
1 tablespoon garlic powder
1 teaspoon allspice
1 teaspoon ancho chile powder, or chile powder
   of your choice
Pepper

Finishing Ingredients

For the Pico de Gallo
1 avocado, diced
1 clove garlic, minced
1 lime, juiced
1 small red onion, diced
2 serrano peppers, deseeded and diced
2 small tomatoes, diced
2 tablespoon olive oil
2 tablespoons chopped fresh cilantro
2 tablespoons chopped fresh parsley
Salt and pepper

A fresh pico de gallo salsa is a great way to lighten up a usually heavy steak. It is especially good in summer when the ingredients are fresh from the garden. If you have different herbs on hand feel free to substitute them in. Sweet bell peppers are also very good in this salsa.

Pre-Bath

Mix the spices together in a bowl. Pepper the meat then sprinkle it with the spices. Place in the sous vide pouch and seal.

At this point you can store the pouch in the refrigerator for up to 2 days, freeze it for up to 6 months or cook it right away.

Cooking

Preheat the water bath to 131°F / 55°C.

Place the sous vide pouch in the water bath and cook for the amount of time indicated in the "Cooking by Thickness" section for the time for heating beef from the refrigerator or freezer.

Finishing

Preheat a pan to medium-high heat or a grill to high heat.

Place all of the pico de gallo ingredients in a bowl and mix well.

Take the steak out of the pouches and pat dry. Sear it until browned, about 1 to 2 minutes per side. Remove from the heat and serve with the pico de gallo on the side.

Beef Fajitas

Pre-Bath Time: 15 Minutes
Cooking Time: See "Cooking by Thickness"
Finishing Time: 30 Minutes
Temperature: 131°F / 55°C
Serves: 4 to 6

Pre-Bath Ingredients

For the Steak
1-2 pounds ribeye, preferably 1" or less thick
1 teaspoon ground cumin
1 teaspoon ground coriander
1 teaspoon garlic powder
½ teaspoon ancho chile powder
Pepper

Finishing Ingredients

For the Peppers and Onions
2 tablespoons canola oil
3 cloves garlic, diced
2 onions, preferably vidalia or sweet, cut into ½"
   slices
3 bell peppers - green and red, cut into ¼" strips
1-2 poblano peppers, cut into ¼" strips
Salt and pepper

For the Garnish
10 tortilla wrappers
6 cups sliced lettuce
4 tomatoes, diced
Refried beans
Mexican rice
Grated pepper jack cheese
Sour cream

Fajitas are a hearty middle of the week meal that don't take too much effort. We cook the steak by thickness and then serve it with sauteed peppers and onion. We also list some other common fajita sides but you can use whatever you like in your fajitas.

Pre-Bath

Mix the spices together in a bowl. Pepper the meat then sprinkle it with the spices. Place in the sous vide pouch and seal.

At this point you can store the pouch in the refrigerator for up to 2 days, freeze it for up to 6 months or cook it right away.

Cooking

Preheat the water bath to 131°F / 55°C.

Place the sous vide pouch in the water bath and cook for the amount of time indicated in the "Cooking by Thickness" section for the time for heating beef from the refrigerator or freezer.

Finishing

Heat a pan to medium-high heat.

Add the onion to the pan and cook until it starts to become tender, 5 to 7 minutes. Add the garlic, bell peppers, and poblano peppers and cook until they become tender. Remove from the heat and set aside.

Take the steak out of the pouch and pat dry with a paper towel or dish towel. Sear it for 1 to 2 minutes per side. Remove from the heat.

Slice the steak on the bias and serve with the onion and peppers, tortilla wrappers, and any of the other sides you want.

CHICKEN WITH SPICY MANGO COLESLAW

Pre-Bath Time: 15 Minutes
Cooking Time: See "Cooking by Thickness"
Finishing Time: 30 Minutes
Temperature: 141°F / 60.5°C
Serves: 4

Pre-Bath Ingredients

For the Chicken
4 boneless, skinless chicken breasts, trimmed to
    be under 1" thick
1 teaspoon dried oregano
1 teaspoon ground cumin
1 teaspoon chipotle chile powder, or chile
    powder of your choice
Pepper

Finishing Ingredients

For the Coleslaw
2 tablespoons olive oil
1 lime, juiced
1 or 2 jalapenos, deseeded and diced
¼ red onion, diced
1 cup shredded red cabbage
1 cup shredded green cabbage
1 mango, peeled and diced
2 tablespoons chopped mint
1 teaspoon ground cinnamon
Salt and pepper

*One great way to pump up the taste of chicken breasts
is with flavorful sides. This crunchy coleslaw is a
mixture of sweet and spicy that adds a great flavor to
the chicken as well as wonderful textures.*

Pre-Bath

Mix the spices together in a bowl. Pepper
the chicken then sprinkle with the spices.
Place in the sous vide pouch and seal.

At this point you can store the pouch in the
refrigerator for up to 2 days, freeze it for up
to 6 months or cook it right away. If you
freeze the pouch be sure to thaw it in the
refrigerator for 1 to 2 days before cooking or
increase the cooking time to compensate.

Cooking

Preheat the water bath to 141°F / 60.5°C.

Place the sous vide pouch in the water bath
and cook for the amount of time indicated in
the "Cooking by Thickness" section for the
time for pasteurizing chicken from the
refrigerator to the temperature you are
cooking at.

Finishing

Preheat a pan to medium-high heat.

Place all of the coleslaw ingredients in a
bowl and mix well.

Take the chicken out of the pouches and pat
dry. Sear them for 1 to 2 minutes per side,
just until they brown. Remove from the heat
and serve with the spicy mango coleslaw.

BBQ Chicken Breasts

Pre-Bath Time: 15 Minutes
Cooking Time: See "Cooking by Thickness"
Finishing Time: 15 Minutes
Temperature: 141°F / 60.5°C
Serves: 4

Pre-Bath Ingredients
For the Chicken
4 chicken breasts, whole or butterflied
1 tablespoon garlic powder
3 sprigs of thyme
Pepper

Finishing Ingredients
1-2 cups BBQ sauce

These chicken breasts are great for a fast and flavorful meal and take very little time to prepare or finish. Just serve these with a side salad, some potato salad, or even some mac and cheese. If you have some good rolls or buns on hand this chicken is also great in a hot sandwich, especially with some melted cheddar cheese on them.

Pre-Bath
Pepper the chicken then sprinkle with the garlic powder. Place in the sous vide pouch with the thyme and seal.

At this point you can store the pouch in the refrigerator for up to 2 days, freeze it for up to 6 months or cook it right away. If you freeze the pouch be sure to thaw it in the refrigerator for 1 to 2 days before cooking or increase the cooking time to compensate.

Cooking
Preheat the water bath to 141°F / 60.5°C.

Place the sous vide pouch in the water bath and cook for the amount of time indicated in the "Cooking by Thickness" section for the time for pasteurizing chicken from the refrigerator to the temperature you are cooking at.

Finishing
Heat a grill to high-heat. You won't be cooking the chicken long on it, just searing them, so use the hottest setting.

Remove the chicken from the pouch, pat dry with a paper towel, and place on a plate. Smear a light layer of the BBQ sauce on the chicken then place on the grill and cook for 1 to 2 minutes, until the sauce starts to blacken .

Remove the chicken from the grill, smear another light layer of BBQ sauce on them and serve with the rest of the sauce on the side.

SALMON WITH CUCUMBER-DILL SALAD

Pre-Bath Time: 10 Minutes
Cooking Time: 15 to 30 Minutes
Finishing Time: 20 Minutes
Temperature: 122°F / 50°C for sushi quality or
132°F / 55.6°C otherwise
Serves: 4

Pre-Bath Ingredients
For the Salmon
4 salmon portions
Salt and pepper

Finishing Ingredients
For the Salad
1 cucumber, seeded and diced
3 tablespoons chopped fresh dill
1 teaspoon capers
12-15 cherry tomatoes, halved
1 tablespoon balsamic vinegar
2 tablespoons olive oil
Salt and pepper

Sous vide salmon is a classic recipe and here we complement it with a cucumber and dill salad. The balsamic vinegar will give it some extra sweetness and tartness helping the salmon to shine through.

Pre-Bath
Salt and pepper the salmon, add to the sous vide pouch, and seal.

At this point you can store the pouch in the refrigerator for up to 2 days, freeze it for up to 6 months or cook it right away. If you freeze the pouch be sure to thaw it in the refrigerator for 1 to 2 days before cooking or increase the cooking time to compensate.

Cooking
Preheat the water bath to 122°F / 50°C for sushi quality or 132°F / 55.6°C otherwise.

Place the sous vide pouch in the water bath and cook for 15 to 30 minutes.

Finishing
Preheat a pan to medium-high heat.

To make the salad place all of the salad ingredients in a bowl and stir to thoroughly combine.

Take the salmon out of the pouch and pat dry. Sear it until browned, about 1 minute per side. Place the salmon on a plate and top with a spoonful or two of the salad.

Lemon-Tarragon Swordfish

Pre-Bath Time: 10 Minutes
Cooking Time: 15 to 30 Minutes
Finishing Time: 15 Minutes
Temperature: 122°F / 50°C for sushi quality or
132°F / 55.6°C otherwise
Serves: 2

Pre-Bath Ingredients
For the Swordfish
2 swordfish portions
1 tablespoon butter
Salt and pepper

Finishing Ingredients
For the Butter
½ stick butter, softened at room temperature
2 tablespoons finely chopped fresh tarragon
1 teaspoon grated lemon zest
⅛ teaspoon ground black pepper

The flavor of the swordfish is brightened by the lemon-tarragon butter and it is also a very quick and easy dish to make. This dish is great with steamed vegetables or a light risotto.

Note: You can save extra time by doubling or tripling the butter recipe and storing the extra in the freezer where it will last several months. A good way to store it is to roll it up into a cylinder shape with wax paper. You can then just cut off a disk when you want to use it.

Pre-Bath
Salt and pepper the swordfish then add to the sous vide pouch. Add the unseasoned butter then seal.

At this point you can store the pouch in the refrigerator for up to 2 days, freeze it for up to 6 months or cook it right away. If you freeze the pouch be sure to thaw it in the refrigerator for 1 to 2 days before cooking or increase the cooking time to compensate.

Cooking
Preheat the water bath to 122°F / 50°C for sushi quality or 132°F / 55.6°C otherwise.

Place the sous vide pouch in the water bath and cook for 15 to 30 minutes.

Finishing
Preheat a pan to medium-high heat.

Make the butter by placing all of the butter ingredients in a bowl and mix and mash them together thoroughly using a fork.

Take the swordfish out of the pouch and pat dry. Sear it until just browned, about 1 to 2 minutes per side. Place the swordfish on a plate and place a dollop or two of the butter on top.

RED SNAPPER TOSTADAS

Pre-Bath Time: 10 Minutes
Cooking Time: 10 to 30 Minutes
Finishing Time: 30 Minutes
Temperature: 122°F / 50°C for sushi quality or
132°F / 55.6°C otherwise
Serves: 4

Pre-Bath Ingredients
For the Fish
1 pound red snapper filets
2 teaspoons garlic powder
½ teaspoon cumin
½ teaspoon coriander
Salt and pepper

Finishing Ingredients
For the Salsa
1 avocado, diced
1 mango, diced
1 jalapeno chile, diced
½ cucumber, diced
¼ red onion, diced
2 tablespoons lime juice
2 tablespoons olive oil
2 tablespoons chopped fresh basil
2 tablespoons chopped fresh oregano
Salt and pepper

For the Tostadas
4 flour tortillas

*I love the crunch of tostadas and frying them doesn't
add too much to the cooking time and can be done
while the fish cooks. To test if the oil is hot enough I
will usually have a spare tortilla around that I can rip
pieces off of and add to the oil. They should puff and
turn brown pretty quickly. Of course, if you don't
want to take the effort you can always use the tortillas
as they are.*

Pre-Bath
Mix together the spices in a bowl. Salt and
pepper the snapper then sprinkle with the
spices. Place in the sous vide pouches and
seal.

At this point you can store the pouch in the
refrigerator for up to 2 days, freeze it for up
to 6 months or cook it right away. If you
freeze the pouch be sure to thaw it in the
refrigerator for 1 to 2 days before cooking or
increase the cooking time to compensate.

Cooking
Preheat the water bath to 122°F / 50°C for
sushi quality or 132°F / 55.6°C otherwise.

Place the sous vide pouch in the water bath
and cook for 10 to 30 minutes.

Finishing
To make the salsa combine all of the
ingredients in a bowl and mix well.

Take a pan large enough to fit one of the
tortillas and heat it over medium to
medium-high heat with about ½" of oil in it.
One at a time place a tortilla in the pan and
cook until it turns a golden brown then
remove from the heat and set on a paper
towel or wire rack. Repeat for all 4 tortillas.

Remove the snapper from the water bath
and pat dry. Serve it on the tostadas with the
salsa.

BLACKENED MAHI MAHI

Pre-Bath Time: 15 Minutes
Cooking Time: 10 to 30 Minutes
Finishing Time: 15 Minutes
Temperature: 122°F / 50°C for sushi quality or
132°F / 55.6°C otherwise
Serves: 2

Pre-Bath Ingredients
2 mahi mahi portions
Salt and pepper

For the Rub
1 tablespoon paprika
1 tablespoon garlic powder
½ teaspoon dried oregano
¼ teaspoon ground cumin
¼ teaspoon cayenne pepper, or to taste
¼ teaspoon dried thyme
½ teaspoon onion powder

Finishing Ingredients
None

*Blackening fish is a great way to add flavor to them.
We make a savory and smoky rub that improves the
taste of the fish and also takes on color very quickly
when it is seared.*

Pre-Bath
First make your rub by combining all the
ingredients in a bowl and stir or whisk to
mix. Any left over rub can be stored in a jar
or tupperware container for several months
in a cabinet.

Salt and pepper the mahi mahi then sprinkle
the on both sides with half of the rub. Place
in the sous vide pouches, and seal.

At this point you can store the pouch in the
refrigerator for up to 2 days, freeze it for up
to 6 months or cook it right away. If you
freeze the pouch be sure to thaw it in the
refrigerator for 1 to 2 days before cooking or
increase the cooking time to compensate.

Cooking
Preheat the water bath to 122°F / 50°C for
sushi quality or 132°F / 55.6°C otherwise.

Place the sous vide pouch in the water bath
and cook for 10 to 30 minutes.

Finishing
Preheat a pan to medium-high heat.

Remove the mahi mahi from the water bath
and pat dry. Sprinkle with the remaining
rub. Sear in the hot pan, about 1 or 2
minutes per side. Remove from the heat and
serve.

SMOKED COD CHOWDER

Pre-Bath Time: 15 Minutes
Cooking Time: 15 to 30 Minutes
Finishing Time: 30 to 45 Minutes
Temperature: 122°F / 50°C for sushi quality or
132°F / 55.6°C otherwise
Serves: 4 to 6

Pre-Bath Ingredients
For the Cod
1 pound cod
2 teaspoons garlic powder
1 teaspoon paprika
1 teaspoon liquid smoke
Salt and pepper

Finishing Ingredients
For the Chowder
4 strips bacon, diced
1 red potato, diced
1 yellow onion, diced
1 carrot, peeled and diced
2 cloves garlic, coarsely chopped
2 tablespoons flour
1 teaspoon yellow mustard
½ teaspoon Worcester sauce
1 cup milk
3 cups fish stock
3 tablespoons fresh parsley

I like a good thick chowder, especially when it has tender seafood in it. Here we use some liquid smoke and paprika to flavor the cod while it's cooking. The chowder itself is a simple mixture of aromatics, milk, and fish stock. You can add more or less flour or fish stock to control the thickness of the chowder. For an even richer chowder you can substitute some of the milk with heavy cream.

Pre-Bath
Salt and pepper the cod then sprinkle with the spices. Brush the liquid smoke on it. Place in the sous vide pouch and seal.

At this point you can store the pouch in the refrigerator for up to 2 days, freeze it for up to 6 months or cook it right away. If you freeze the pouch be sure to thaw it in the refrigerator for 1 to 2 days before cooking or increase the cooking time to compensate.

Cooking
Preheat the water bath to 122°F / 50°C for sushi quality or 132°F / 55.6°C otherwise.

Place the sous vide pouch in the water bath and cook for 15 to 30 minutes.

Finishing
Preheat a pot to medium-high heat.

Add the bacon to the pot and cook until the fat is rendered and it begins to crisp up. Remove the bacon and set aside, discarding all but 1 tablespoon of bacon fat. Add the potato, onion, carrot, and garlic to the pot and cook until the potato begins to turn tender. Add the flour, mustard, and Worcester sauce and mix well. Slowly whisk in the milk and half of the fish stock. Bring to a simmer and continue whisking in fish stock until it is the consistency you prefer.

Remove the cod from the water bath and cut into portions. Spoon the soup into bowls and top with the cod, the reserved bacon, and the parsley.

Sea Bass with Radishes and Tomatoes

Pre-Bath Time: 10 Minutes
Cooking Time: 15 to 30 Minutes
Finishing Time: 25 Minutes
Temperature: 122°F / 50°C for sushi quality or
132°F / 55.6°C otherwise
Serves: 4

Pre-Bath Ingredients

For the Sea bass
4 sea bass portions
1 tablespoon butter
Salt and pepper

Finishing Ingredients

For the Salad
6 radishes, thinly sliced
12 cherry tomatoes, halved
2 tablespoons chopped fresh mint
2 tablespoons orange juice
2 tablespoons olive oil
Salt and pepper

Sea bass comes out nice and light when cooked sous vide. We pair it with a salad of radish, tomato, and mint to complement it. I give directions for searing the fish but it is also very good when eaten straight from the sous vide pouch.

Pre-Bath

Salt and pepper the sea bass then add to the sous vide pouch. Add the butter and seal.

At this point you can store the pouch in the refrigerator for up to 2 days, freeze it for up to 6 months or cook it right away. If you freeze the pouch be sure to thaw it in the refrigerator for 1 to 2 days before cooking or increase the cooking time to compensate.

Cooking

Preheat the water bath to 122°F / 50°C for sushi quality or 132°F / 55.6°C otherwise.

Place the sous vide pouch in the water bath and cook for 15 to 30 minutes.

Finishing

Preheat a pan to medium-high heat or a grill to high heat.

To make the salad place all of the salad ingredients in a bowl and stir well to combine.

Take the sea bass out of the pouch and pat dry. Sear it until just browned, about 1 minute per side. Place the sea bass on a plate and place a spoonful or two of the salad on top.

MOROCCAN GROUPER WITH CHICKPEAS

Pre-Bath Time: 15 Minutes
Cooking Time: 10 to 30 Minutes
Finishing Time: 25 Minutes
Temperature: 122°F / 50°C for sushi quality or
132°F / 55.6°C otherwise
Serves: 2

Pre-Bath Ingredients

For the Fish
4 grouper filets, cleaned
½ teaspoon paprika
½ teaspoon ginger
½ teaspoon cumin
⅛ teaspoon turmeric
2 tablespoons butter or olive oil
Salt and pepper

Finishing Ingredients

For the Chickpeas
1 can of chickpeas, rinsed and drained
½ red bell pepper, diced
4 cloves garlic, minced
1 tablespoon ground cumin
1 tablespoon olive oil
¼ teaspoon cayenne pepper or chile pepper of
     your choice

This dish combines many of the flavors of traditional Moroccan cuisine into a rub for the grouper. I tend not to sear the fish before serving but if you want some extra flavor and texture you can sear it. The chickpeas add some flavor and texture without overpowering the grouper.

Pre Bath

Combine all the spices in a bowl. Salt and pepper the grouper and then sprinkle with the spice mixture. Add to the sous vide pouches along with the butter then seal.

At this point you can store the pouch in the refrigerator for up to 2 days, freeze it for up to 6 months or cook it right away. If you freeze the pouch be sure to thaw it in the refrigerator for 1 to 2 days before cooking or increase the cooking time to compensate.

Cooking

Preheat the water bath to 122°F / 50°C for sushi quality or 132°F / 55.6°C otherwise.

Place the sous vide pouch in the water bath and cook for 10 to 30 minutes.

Finishing

Make the chickpeas by combining all of the ingredients and mixing well.

Take the fish out of the sous vide bath and place on individual plates. Top with a spoonful of the juices from the pouch and the chickpeas.

FISH TACOS WITH CORN SALSA

Pre-Bath Time: 15 Minutes
Cooking Time: 10 to 30 Minutes
Finishing Time: 25 Minutes
Temperature: 122°F / 50°C for sushi quality or
132°F / 55.6°C otherwise
Serves: 4

Pre-Bath Ingredients
For the Fish
1 pound mahi mahi
2 teaspoons garlic powder
½ teaspoon paprika
¼ teaspoon chipotle powder, or chile powder of
    your choice
Salt and pepper

Finishing Ingredients
For the Corn Salsa
1 cup corn kernels, cooked
2 tomatoes, diced
1 avocado, diced
½ cup black beans, either canned or cooked
2 tablespoons chopped red onion
¼ cup fresh cilantro
4 cloves garlic, diced
2 tablespoons olive oil
1 teaspoon lime juice

For the Tacos
4-6 soft corn tortillas

*These fish tacos are inspired by some that my friend
made when I was out visiting them in Denver.
Avocado and corn always go great together and they
form the base for this flavorful salsa. If you can't find
mahi mahi you can use any flaky, white fish.*

Pre-Bath
Mix the spices together in a bowl. Salt and pepper the mahi mahi then sprinkle with the spices. Place in the sous vide pouches and seal.

At this point you can store the pouch in the refrigerator for up to 2 days, freeze it for up to 6 months or cook it right away. If you freeze the pouch be sure to thaw it in the refrigerator for 1 to 2 days before cooking or increase the cooking time to compensate.

Cooking
Preheat the water bath to 122°F / 50°C for sushi quality or 132°F / 55.6°C otherwise.

Place the sous vide pouch in the water bath and cook for 10 to 30 minutes.

Finishing
To make the salsa combine all of the ingredients in a bowl and mix well.

Remove the mahi mahi from the water bath and pat dry. Serve it with the salsa and the corn tortillas.

SHRIMP POMODORO OVER LINGUINE

Pre-Bath Time: 15 Minutes
Cooking Time: 15 to 35 Minutes
Finishing Time: 30 Minutes
Temperature: 122°F / 50°C for sushi quality or
132°F / 55.6°C otherwise
Serves: 4

Pre-Bath Ingredients
For the Shrimp
20-25 medium sized shrimp, shelled and
  deveined
1 tablespoon butter
¼ teaspoon cayenne pepper, or chile powder of
  your choice
Salt and pepper

Finishing Ingredients
12 ounces linguine pasta, or pasta of your choice

For the Pomodoro Sauce
2 tablespoons olive oil
4 cloves garlic, minced
½ yellow onion, diced
1 28-ounce can of diced tomatoes
1 tablespoon butter
2 tablespoons chopped fresh basil
1 tablespoon chopped fresh oregano
Salt and pepper

For the Garnish
Parmesan cheese
1 tablespoon chopped basil
1 tablespoon lemon zest

*Pomodoro sauce is a very fast tomato sauce to make. It
really highlights the flavor of the tomatoes and herbs
in it. I like to serve this with some fresh bread to really
soak up all the sauce.*

*Here I call for using canned, diced tomatoes which
work well but if you have some extra time there's
nothing like fresh tomatoes in the middle of summer.
Just dice them and cook them for an extra 5 minutes
when you add them to the dish to break them down.*

Pre-Bath
Salt and pepper the shrimp, sprinkle with
the cayenne pepper, then add to the sous
vide pouch in a single layer. Add the butter
and seal.

At this point you can store the pouch in the
refrigerator for up to 2 days, freeze it for up
to 6 months or cook it right away. If you
freeze the pouch be sure to thaw it in the
refrigerator for 1 to 2 days before cooking or
increase the cooking time to compensate.

Cooking
Preheat the water bath to 122°F / 50°C for
sushi quality or 132°F / 55.6°C otherwise.

Place the sous vide pouch in the water bath
and cook for 15 to 35 minutes.

Finishing
Bring a pot of salted water to a boil. Heat a
pan over medium to medium-high heat.

Add the linguine to the water and cook until
tender.

Meanwhile, make the pomodoro sauce. Add
the olive oil to the pan and heat. Cook the
garlic for 1 minute then add the onion and
cook until it begins to soften and turn
translucent. Add the tomatoes and some of
their juices to the pan and cook for 5 to 10
minutes. Whisk in the butter, add the basil
and oregano, salt and pepper to taste, then
mix well.

Spoon the pasta into bowls and top with the
pomodoro sauce. Take the shrimp out of the
pouches and place on top of the pasta. Grate
the parmesan cheese on top and sprinkle
with the basil and lemon zest.

SHRIMP SALAD

Pre-Bath Time: 10 Minutes
Cooking Time: 15 to 35 Minutes
Finishing Time: 20 Minutes
Temperature: 122°F / 50°C for sushi quality or
132°F / 55.6°C otherwise
Serves: 4

Pre-Bath Ingredients

For the Shrimp
1 pound shrimp, shelled and deveined
1 tablespoon butter
Salt and pepper

Finishing Ingredients

For the Dressing
1 tablespoon lemon juice
¼ cup mayonnaise
3 tablespoons chopped fresh parsley
3 tablespoons chopped fresh basil
¼ teaspoon chipotle chile powder, or chile
  powder of your choice
Salt and pepper

For the Salad
1 cup cooked corn kernels
1 celery stalk, finely diced
1 red pepper, diced
Salt and pepper

*This is a great replacement for the shrimp salads you
find at grocery stores. The dressing is nice and light
and just coats the salad without overwhelming it. You
can serve this salad on the side of a large dish, on
lettuce by itself, or even in a roll as a great sandwich.*

*I usually use smaller shrimp or cut medium ones into
bite-sized pieces. However, it can be a dramatic
presentation if larger, whole shrimp are used.*

Pre-Bath

Salt and pepper the shrimp then add to the
sous vide pouch in a single layer. Add the
butter then seal.

At this point you can store the pouch in the
refrigerator for up to 2 days, freeze it for up
to 6 months or cook it right away. If you
freeze the pouch be sure to thaw it in the
refrigerator for 1 to 2 days before cooking or
increase the cooking time to compensate.

Cooking

Preheat the water bath to 122°F / 50°C for
sushi quality or 132°F / 55.6°C otherwise.

Place the sous vide pouch in the water bath
and cook for 15 to 35 minutes.

Finishing

To make the dressing mix together all of the
ingredients in a bowl until thoroughly
combined.

Remove the shrimp from the sous vide bags
and coarsely chop. Add to the dressing
along with the corn, celery, and red pepper.
Salt and pepper to taste and serve.

Spicy Corn and Mango Salad With Shrimp

Pre-Bath Time: 15 Minutes
Cooking Time: 15 to 35 Minutes
Finishing Time: 30 Minutes
Temperature: 122°F / 50°C for sushi quality or
132°F / 55.6°C otherwise
Serves: 4

Pre-Bath Ingredients
For the Shrimp
1 pound shrimp, shelled and deveined
1 tablespoon paprika
Salt and pepper

Finishing Ingredients
For the Salad
1-4 tablespoons habanero-mango hot sauce, or
 hot sauce of your choice
1 tablespoon white wine vinegar
2 tablespoons olive oil
2 cups cooked corn kernels
1 red bell pepper, diced
1 mango, diced
1 handful red and green lettuce
12 cherry tomatoes, halved
1 handful fresh basil, chopped
1 tablespoon lemon zest
Salt and pepper

I love eating shrimp prepared just about any way imaginable. I love them poached and grilled and in ceviche and everything in between. When I was at the fish market they had some great looking shrimp so I decided to grab some with no plan in mind. Once I got home I checked to see what we had on hand and I came up with this salad.

It would also be great with a white fish like cod, swordfish, or grouper. Even chicken breasts would go well with it.

Pre-Bath
Salt and pepper the shrimp and sprinkle with the paprika. Add to the sous vide pouch in a single layer and seal.

At this point you can store the pouch in the refrigerator for up to 2 days, freeze it for up to 6 months or cook it right away. If you freeze the pouch be sure to thaw it in the refrigerator for 1 to 2 days before cooking or increase the cooking time to compensate.

Cooking
Preheat the water bath to 122°F / 50°C for sushi quality or 132°F / 55.6°C otherwise.

Place the sous vide pouch in the water bath and cook for 15 to 35 minutes.

Finishing
While the sous vide shrimp are cooking make the salad. Whisk together the hot sauce, vinegar, and olive oil in a large bowl. Add the corn, pepper, and mango and mix well. Salt and pepper to taste.

Place the lettuce in individual bowls and add the corn mixture. Place the cherry tomatoes on top of the salad.

Remove the shrimp from the sous vide bags and add to the top of the salads. Top with the basil and lemon zest then serve.

SCALLOPS WITH MANGO AND MINT

Pre-Bath Time: 15 Minutes
Cooking Time: 15 to 35 Minutes
Finishing Time: 20 Minutes
Temperature: 122°F / 50°C
Serves: 4

Pre-Bath Ingredients
For the Scallops
1 pound large scallops
1 tablespoon butter
Salt and pepper

Finishing Ingredients
For the Sauce
1 tablespoon orange juice
2 tablespoons olive oil
Salt and pepper

For the Garnish
1 tablespoon lime zest
1 tablespoon orange zest
1 cup diced mango
1 serrano pepper, thinly sliced
2 tablespoons chopped mint leaves

Sous vide scallops take on an interesting texture that you don't get just from searing them. The sous vide lightly cooks them and then the searing finishes them off. We pair them with a sweet garnish of mango, mint, and a little hot pepper.

Pre-Bath

Salt and pepper the scallops then add to the sous vide pouch in a single layer. Add the butter then seal.

At this point you can store the pouch in the refrigerator for up to 2 days, freeze it for up to 6 months or cook it right away. If you freeze the pouch be sure to thaw it in the refrigerator for 1 to 2 days before cooking or increase the cooking time to compensate.

Cooking

Preheat the water bath to 122°F / 50°C.

Place the sous vide pouch in the water bath and cook for 15 to 35 minutes.

Finishing

Heat a pan over medium to medium-high heat.

To make the sauce whisk together all of the ingredients in a bowl until thoroughly combined.

Remove the scallops from the sous vide bags and pat dry. Sear in the pan on one side until they just begin to brown. Remove from the heat and place on a plate with the browned side up.

Drizzle the scallops with the sauce and top with the garnishes.

TURKEY CUTLETS WITH MINT AND PEA PESTO

Pre-Bath Time: 15 Minutes
Cooking Time: See "Cooking by Thickness"
Finishing Time: 30 Minutes
Temperature: 141°F / 60.5°C
Serves: 4

Pre-Bath Ingredients

For the Turkey
1 pound turkey cutlets
2 teaspoons garlic powder
1 teaspoon onion powder
Pepper

Finishing Ingredients

For the Pesto
2 cups frozen peas
1 cup packed fresh spinach
½ cup pecans
¼ cup water
2 cloves garlic, roughly chopped
8-12 mint leaves
½ cup olive oil
3 tablespoons parmesan cheese
Salt and pepper

Turkey is often bland and overcooked. Using sous vide keeps it warm and this unusual pesto adds a lot of flavor to it. Mint and peas go together very well and the turkey is a great way to showcase them.

Pre-Bath

Pepper the turkey then sprinkle with the spices. Place in the sous vide pouch and seal.

At this point you can store the pouch in the refrigerator for up to 2 days, freeze it for up to 6 months or cook it right away. If you freeze the pouch be sure to thaw it in the refrigerator for 1 to 2 days before cooking or increase the cooking time to compensate.

Cooking

Preheat the water bath to 141°F / 60.5°C.

Place the sous vide pouch in the water bath and cook for the amount of time indicated in the "Cooking by Thickness" section for the time for pasteurizing chicken from the refrigerator to the temperature you are cooking at.

Finishing

To make the pesto put the peas, spinach, pecans, water, garlic, and mint into a food processor and process until well mixed. Add the olive oil and process until it is all incorporated. Stir in the parmesan cheese.

Take the turkey out of the sous vide pouches and pat dry. Sear for 1 to 2 minutes per side, just until browned.

Serve the turkey cutlets with a dollop of pesto on top.

COOK, CHILL, AND HOLD

Interested in sous vide shirts, aprons, and mugs?
We have a bunch of different gear you can buy in our online store.

You can find the sous vide gear at:
www.zazzle.com/cooking_sous_vide

GENERAL PROCESS

Cook, chill, and hold is a great technique for people to use in their menu planning. Being able to cook the food at one time and then eat it at another, with no loss in quality, is a great way to work around a busy schedule.

Cook, chill, and hold can be used on almost any kind of food but in this chapter we focus mainly on foods that are cooked for 2 to 8 hours. This is because these foods are hard to cook with sous vide if you are not home several hours before you want to eat.

Pre-Bath Stage

The *Pre-Bath* stage usually will consist of seasoning and bagging the food. Unless you need to cube or trim the meat it is a very quick process. You can do this prep work several days in advance if you are keeping it in the refrigerator or months in advance if you freeze the food once it's been bagged. You can also do it the day it goes into the water bath if that works best for you.

Cooking Stage

The cooking stage will last for a variable amount of time and can be done whenever you have time.

Once the cooking is done you move the food directly into a bowl filled with ½ ice and ½ water. The food should stay there until it is completely chilled.

In general, it takes food the same amount of time to cool as it does to heat. A good guide is to look at the Beef, Pork, Lamb Thickness Chart in the "Cooking By Thickness" section to see how long it takes. The chicken tables take into account the time of pasteurization which isn't needed during chilling.

This chilling process is critical to the safety of the food. The less time the food is in the danger zone of 40°F to 130°F (4°C to 54°C) the less time any bacteria can grow.

Finishing Stage

The Finishing stage will generally start with bringing the food back up to temperature on the night you want to eat. This can be accomplished in a variety of ways from placing it in the water bath to searing it for a longer amount of time.

The food is already completely cooked so you don't have to heat it to the exact temperature you want it cooked to. Once the food is back up to temperature you finish the meal and are ready to eat.

In the following recipes we sometimes recommend a way of bringing the food back up to temperature but in general you can use whichever method you feel most comfortable with.

COOK, CHILL, AND HOLD MEATS

You can use cook, chill, and hold with almost any type of meat or fish with good results.

TIPS AND TRICKS

Reheat to a Lower Temperature

If you use the water bath to bring the food back up to temperature before searing it I recommend only heating it to the minimum safe temperature. This gives you more leeway for searing without overcooking the food.

For beef and pork I recommend 131°F / 55°C and for poultry I suggest 136°F /

57.7°C. And remember, since the food is already cooked you won't have "underdone" food since this is just reheating it.

Reheat by Searing for More Crust

How you reheat your food depends on the recipe and your personal preference. Any recipes will be fine if you reheat the food using your water bath to the original temperature. However, I sometimes like to reheat food, especially thick food, by searing it. While this sacrifices some of the "perfect" middle I find the extra sear makes up for it.

Sear to a Lower Temperature

When reheating your food by searing it there's no reason to sear it to the final temperature. Doing that defeats the process of using sous vide in the first place. When searing only cook the food until the middle is warm (about 115 for steaks) and you won't have much of a gray ring while getting a lot better crust. Remember, the food is already cooked so you just need it hot enough to be tasty.

Use a Thermometer

To make sure you don't overcook your food when you are reheating by searing I recommend using a thermometer to monitor the internal temperature.

Don't Double Freeze

In general, we recommend against freezing the food after both the *Pre-Bath* stage and *Cooking* stage. Try to only freeze at one or the other to keep the quality of the food high.

Reheat in the Sauce

Many dishes such as curries, stews, and chilies contain a thick sauce. You can reheat the meat in the sauce in order to infuse it with even more flavor. Just be careful to only leave the meat in until it gets warm before serving it. You don't want to cook the meat any further than it already is.

Make Extras

One easy way to speed up your weekday cooking is to make an extra package or two of meat and then freeze it after it is chilled. That way you can make the dish later and only have to reheat the meat before finishing the meal.

Ribeye with Red Wine Mushrooms

Pre-Bath Time: 15 Minutes
Cooking Time: 2 to 8 Hours
Finishing Time: 45 Minutes
Temperature: 131°F / 55°C
Serves: 4

Pre-Bath Ingredients
For the Steak
1-2 pounds sirloin steak
1 teaspoon dried thyme
1 teaspoon garlic powder
Pepper

Finishing Ingredients
For the Red Wine Mushrooms
1 tablespoon olive oil
1 package baby bella mushrooms, sliced
1 shallot, minced
1 clove garlic, minced
½ cup red wine
1 tablespoon balsamic vinegar
½ teaspoon Dijon mustard
2 tablespoons butter, cut into large pieces
1 teaspoon fresh thyme
1 tablespoon chopped fresh parsley
Salt and pepper

I love a good steak and these red wine mushrooms add a lot to the overall flavor of the dish without taking a long time to put together. This pan sauce can be used with beef roasts.

Note: If desired, reheat the food in the water bath at the beginning of the Finishing stage. Otherwise add a few minutes to the searing time for the middle to warm.

Pre-Bath
Pepper the meat then sprinkle with the garlic and thyme. Add to the sous vide pouches and seal.

At this point you can store the pouch in the refrigerator for up to 2 days, freeze it for up to 6 months, or cook it right away.

Cooking
Preheat the water bath to 131°F / 55°C. Place the sous vide pouches in the water bath and cook for 2 to 8 hours.

Remove the pouches and place in a ½ ice - ½ water bath until chilled. You can store the pouches in the refrigerator for around 2 days or freeze them for up to 6 months.

Finishing
Heat a pan over medium-high heat or a grill to high heat. Heat another pan over medium-high heat for the mushrooms.

Take the steaks out of the pouches, reserving the juices, and pat dry.

Add the olive oil to the mushroom pan and let warm. Add the mushrooms and cook until tender, 5 to 7 minutes, stirring occasionally. Add the garlic and shallot and cook for 1 minute. Add the red wine and ½ cup of the reserved sous vide juices. Cook until thickened, about 5 minutes. Add the vinegar and mustard and mix well. Stir in the butter, thyme, and parsley, then salt and pepper to taste.

Sear the steaks until browned, about 1 to 2 minutes per side. Spoon the mushrooms and sauce over the steaks then serve.

SPAGHETTI AND MEATBALLS

Pre-Bath Time: 45 Minutes
Cooking Time: 2 to 4 Hours
Finishing Time: 30 to 45 Minutes
Temperature: 131°F / 55°C
Serves: 4

Pre-Bath Ingredients

For the Meatballs
⅔ pound ground beef
⅔ pound ground pork
4 cloves garlic, minced
1 large egg
¼ cup grated parmesan cheese
1 slice of bread, diced
Pepper

Finishing Ingredients

12 ounces spaghetti, or pasta or your choice

For the Marinara Sauce
2 tablespoons olive oil
4 cloves garlic, minced
½ yellow onion, diced
1 red pepper, diced
2 tablespoons tomato paste
1 28-ounce can of crushed tomatoes
2 tablespoons balsamic vinegar

For Garnish
Parmesan cheese
2 tablespoons chopped fresh basil
1 tablespoon chopped fresh oregano

The multiple types of meat in these meatballs add a lot of flavor and depth but you can go with 100% ground beef if you prefer. I prefer a fattier ground beef mix since the fat really adds flavor, if you go with a 90% lean mix they will often turn out a little dry.

To save more time you can use pre-made meatballs that you can often find at the grocery store. You can also use your favorite packaged pasta sauce.

Note: If desired, reheat the food in the water bath at the beginning of the Finishing stage. Otherwise add a few minutes to the searing time for the middle to warm.

Pre-Bath

Place all the ingredients for the meatballs into a large bowl. Using your hands mix them together gently until combined. Form the meat into 2" balls and place into the sous vide pouch. Gently seal the pouch, being careful not to crush the meatballs.

At this point you can store the pouch in the refrigerator for up to 2 days, freeze it for up to 6 months, or cook it right away.

Cooking

Preheat the water bath to 131°F / 55°C. Place the sous vide pouches in the water bath and cook for 2 to 4 hours.

Remove the pouches and place in a ½ ice - ½ water bath until chilled. You can store the pouches in the refrigerator for around 2 days or freeze them for up to 6 months.

Finishing

Preheat a pot or deep pan to medium-high heat. Bring a pot of salted water to a boil.

Add the spaghetti to the water and cook until tender.

Take the meatballs out of the pouches and pat dry. Sear them in the pot until browned on all sides, 1 to 2 minutes per side. Remove from the heat and set aside under foil.

Add the olive oil to the pot and heat. Cook the garlic for 1 minute then add the onion and cook until it begins to soften and turn translucent. Add the pepper and cook for 2 to 3 minutes. Add the tomato paste and cook while stirring for 2 minutes. Add the crushed tomatoes and balsamic vinegar and let simmer for several minutes until it thickens and the flavors come together.

Place the spaghetti in individual bowls and top with a spoonful or two of the marinara sauce. Add a meatball or two to each bowl, grate the parmesan cheese on top, and sprinkle the herbs over everything.

CHICKEN CAPRESE GRINDERS

Pre-Bath Time: 15 Minutes
Cooking Time: 2 to 3 Hours
Finishing Time: 30 Minutes
Temperature: 141°F / 60.5°C
Serves: 4

Pre-Bath Ingredients
For the Sausage
4-6 chicken sausages, about 1" diameter
1 teaspoon sage

Finishing Ingredients
For the Salsa
2 tomatoes, diced
1 bunch basil, chopped
1 tablespoon balsamic vinegar
1 tablespoon olive oil
Pepper

For the Grinders
4 hoagie or sub rolls, cut to hold the sausage
8 slices of fresh mozzarella rounds, ⅛" thick

Basil, tomatoes, and mozzarella are a classic pairing in a caprese salad. Here we turn that salad into a salsa and use it to top chicken sausage that is cooked sous vide and then grilled. I suggest using the sausage directly out of the refrigerator so you can get a better char on the casing.

Pre-Bath
Sprinkle the sausages with the sage and place into the sous vide pouch. Seal the pouch.

At this point you can store the pouch in the refrigerator for up to 2 days, freeze it for up to 6 months, or cook it right away.

Cooking
Preheat the water bath to 141°F / 60.5°C. Place the sous vide pouches in the water bath and cook for 2 to 3 hours.

Remove the pouches and place in a ½ ice - ½ water bath until chilled. You can store the pouches in the refrigerator for around 2 days or freeze them for up to 6 months.

Finishing
Heat a grill to high heat.

While the grill is heating make the salsa. Mix together the tomato, basil, balsamic vinegar, and olive oil in a bowl. Salt and pepper it and mix well.

Place the hoagie rolls cut side down on the grill and cook until they start to brown. Remove from the heat and place the mozzarella cheese on each.

Remove the chicken sausages from their pouches and pat them dry. Sear them on the grill, turning as the casing cooks, until nicely browned and warmed throughout.

Remove from the heat and place on the grilled hoagie rolls. Top with the tomato-basil salsa and serve.

CHICKEN SOFT TACOS

Pre-Bath Time: 15 Minutes
Cooking Time: 2 to 4 Hours
Finishing Time: 30 Minutes
Temperature: 141°F / 60.5°C
Serves: 4

Pre-Bath Ingredients

For the Chicken
1 pound chicken breasts
1 teaspoon ground cumin
1 teaspoon ground coriander
1 teaspoon ancho chile powder, or your chile
    powder of choice
Pepper

Finishing Ingredients

For the Tortillas
8 6-inch flour tortillas
1 cup shredded lettuce
1 tomato, diced
½ cup shredded cheddar cheese
Sour cream
1 lime, quartered

Chicken soft tacos are a great mid-week meal because they come together so fast. You can always sear the chicken for more flavor but I've found the unseared breasts work just fine. You can serve these with any accompaniments you like and often times I'll serve the sides in bowls so each person can make their own tacos they way they like them.

Pre-Bath

Mix the spices together in a bowl. Pepper the chicken then sprinkle with the spice mixture and seal in a sous vide pouch.

At this point you can store the pouch in the refrigerator for up to 2 days, freeze it for up to 6 months, or cook it right away.

Cooking

Preheat the water bath to 141°F / 60.5°C. Place the sous vide pouches in the water bath and cook for 2 to 4 hours.

Remove the pouches and place in a ½ ice - ½ water bath until chilled. You can store the pouches in the refrigerator for around 2 days or freeze them for up to 6 months.

Finishing

Preheat a water bath to 141°F / 60.5°C. Place the chicken in the water bath until it comes back up to temperature, about 30 to 45 minutes.

Remove the chicken from the pouches and cut into ½" strips.

Lay out the tortillas and top each one with the chicken, lettuce, tomato, cheddar cheese and sour cream. Squeeze some lime juice over the top and serve.

CHICKEN TIKKA MASALA

Pre-Bath Time: 15 Minutes
Cooking Time: 2 to 4 Hours
Finishing Time: 45 Minutes
Temperature: 141°F / 60.5°C
Serves: 4

Pre-Bath Ingredients

1 pound chicken breasts
1 teaspoon garlic powder
1 teaspoon ground cumin
1 teaspoon ground coriander
¼ teaspoon cayenne chile powder, or your chile
   powder of choice
Pepper

Finishing Ingredients

For the Masala Sauce
1 onion, diced
3 teaspoons grated fresh ginger
3 cloves garlic, diced
1 serrano chile, deseeded and diced
1 tablespoon tomato paste
2 tablespoons garam masala
1 28-ounce can crushed tomatoes
1 tablespoon honey
1 cup heavy cream
¼ cup chopped cilantro leaves
Salt and pepper

1 cup plain yogurt

*Tikka masala is a traditional English dish at curry
houses. This is a simple sous vide take on it that
brings out the flavors without taking too long to
prepare. For an even simpler version you can take the
chicken out of the sous vide pouches and place it
directly into the sauce without grilling it.*

*For this dish I recommend using the chicken directly
out of the refrigerator. This will allow you to better
sear it with the yogurt without overcooking it. If you
are taking it directly from the water bath just be sure
not to grill it for too long.*

Pre-Bath

Mix the spices together in a bowl. Pepper
the chicken then sprinkle with the spice
mixture and seal in a sous vide pouch.

At this point you can store the pouch in the
refrigerator for up to 2 days, freeze it for up
to 6 months, or cook it right away.

Cooking

Preheat the water bath to 141°F / 60.5°C.
Place the sous vide pouches in the water
bath and cook for 2 to 4 hours.

Remove the pouches and place in a ½ ice - ½
water bath until chilled. You can store the
pouches in the refrigerator for around 2
days or freeze them for up to 6 months.

Finishing

Preheat a grill to high heat.

Heat a pan over medium to medium-high
heat. Add oil and warm. Add the onion and
cook until translucent, about 5 to 7 minutes.
Add the garlic, ginger, and serrano pepper
and cook for 2 minutes.

Add the tomato paste and garam masala
and cook, stirring regularly, for 3 minutes.
Add the crushed tomatoes and honey and
bring to a simmer for around 15 minutes.

Take the chicken out of the sous vide
pouches and coat with the yogurt. Place on
the grill and cook until the center nears
115°F / 46°C, turning once or twice.

Remove the chicken from the heat and cut
into 1" chunks. Add the chicken, heavy
cream, and cilantro to the sauce and mix well.
Remove from the heat and serve in bowls.

SPAGHETTI WITH CHICKEN AND WALNUT SAUCE

Pre-Bath Time: 15 Minutes
Cooking Time: 2 to 4 Hours
Finishing Time: 30 Minutes
Temperature: 141°F / 60.5°C
Serves: 6

Pre-Bath Ingredients

For the Chicken
4 chicken breasts
1 teaspoon garlic powder
1 teaspoon ginger powder
Pepper

Finishing Ingredients

1 pound whole wheat spaghetti, or pasta of your
   choice

For the Walnut Sauce
1 cup walnuts
1 slice bread, crusts removed
⅓ cup whole milk
2 tablespoons heavy cream
2 cloves garlic, coarsely chopped
3 tablespoons olive oil
Salt and pepper

For Garnish
2 tablespoons chopped fresh parsley
2 tablespoons chopped fresh basil
2 tablespoons chopped walnuts
Parmesan cheese

*This walnut sauce is very flavorful and isn't found
too often. For even more flavor you can toast the
walnuts in a dry pan before you add them to the food
processor.*

*Note: If desired, reheat the food in the water bath at
the beginning of the Finishing stage. Otherwise add a
few minutes to the searing time for the middle to
warm.*

Pre-Bath

Mix the spices together in a bowl. Pepper
the chicken then sprinkle with the spice
mixture and seal in a sous vide pouch.

At this point you can store the pouch in the
refrigerator for up to 2 days, freeze it for up
to 6 months, or cook it right away.

Cooking

Preheat the water bath to 141°F / 60.5°C.
Place the sous vide pouches in the water
bath and cook for 2 to 4 hours.

Remove the pouches and place in a ½ ice - ½
water bath until chilled. You can store the
pouches in the refrigerator for around 2
days or freeze them for up to 6 months.

Finishing

Heat a pan over medium-high heat. Bring a
pot of salted water to a boil.

Add the spaghetti to the water and cook
until tender.

Make the walnut sauce by putting all the
ingredients into a blender or food processor
and processing until it forms a smooth, thick
sauce, adding more milk if it is too thick.

Remove the chicken from the water bath
and pat dry. Sear in the pan until just
browned, about 1 or 2 minutes per side.
Remove from the heat and cut into ½" slices.

Place the cooked pasta into a bowl with the
walnut sauce and mix well. Top with the
fresh herbs, walnuts, and chicken. Grate
some fresh parmesan cheese on it and serve.

Orange-Mint Glazed Chicken Thighs

Pre-Bath Time: 15 Minutes
Cooking Time: 2 to 5 Hours
Finishing Time: 15 Minutes
Temperature: 148°F / 64.5°C
Serves: 4

Pre-Bath Ingredients
For the Chicken
1 pound chicken thighs
1 teaspoon garlic powder
1 teaspoon ground coriander
1 teaspoon ancho chile powder, or your chile
  powder of choice
Pepper

Finishing Ingredients
For the Sauce
6 cloves garlic, diced
¼ teaspoon chipotle powder, or chile powder of
  your choice
1½ cups orange juice

For the Garnish
¼ cup chopped mint

These chicken thighs have a great combination of sweet, spicy, and minty flavors. The sauce is very easy to make and is poured directly over the chicken thighs before serving. To help it thicken more quickly you can also add a mixture of ½ cold water and ½ corn starch to it when it is on the stove.

Note: If desired, reheat the food in the water bath at the beginning of the Finishing stage. Otherwise add a few minutes to the searing time for the middle to warm.

Pre-Bath
Mix the spices together in a bowl. Pepper the chicken then sprinkle with the spice mixture and seal in a sous vide pouch.

At this point you can store the pouch in the refrigerator for up to 2 days, freeze it for up to 6 months, or cook it right away.

Cooking
Preheat the water bath to 148°F / 64.5°C. Place the sous vide pouches in the water bath and cook for 2 to 5 hours.

Remove the pouches and place in a ½ ice - ½ water bath until chilled. You can store the pouches in the refrigerator for around 2 days or freeze them for up to 6 months.

Finishing
Heat a pan over medium-high heat.

Remove the chicken from the pouches and pat dry. Sear the chicken in the pan until they begin to brown. Remove from the heat and set on a plate under foil.

Add the garlic to the pan and let cook for about 1 minute. Add the chipotle powder and orange juice and cook until it thickens some, about 10 to 15 minutes.

To serve, place the chicken on plates. Pour the sauce over the chicken and top with the chopped mint.

CHICKEN SALAD WITH BACON-CHIPOTLE RANCH

Pre-Bath Time: 15 Minutes
Cooking Time: 2 to 4 Hours
Finishing Time: 30 Minutes
Temperature: 141°F / 60.5°C
Serves: 4

Pre-Bath Ingredients
For the Chicken
1 pound chicken breasts
1 teaspoon garlic powder
1 teaspoon onion powder
Pepper

Finishing Ingredients
For the Dressing
2 cups ranch dressing
1-2 chipotle peppers in adobo sauce, more or less
  to taste
4 strips of cooked bacon

For the Salad
1 red pepper, cut into strips
1 tomato, diced
8 baby bella or white button mushrooms, sliced
¼ cup sunflower seeds
Mixed greens or the lettuce of your choice

This chicken salad is really kicked up a notch by the bacon and chipotle peppers. The peppers can be very hot so you might want to add them slowly and taste the dressing after each one until it gets to the heat level you like.

Note: If desired, reheat the food in the water bath at the beginning of the Finishing stage. Otherwise add a few minutes to the searing time for the middle to warm.

Pre-Bath
Mix the spices together in a bowl. Pepper the chicken then sprinkle with the spice mixture and seal in a sous vide pouch.

At this point you can store the pouch in the refrigerator for up to 2 days, freeze it for up to 6 months, or cook it right away.

Cooking
Preheat the water bath to 141°F / 60.5°C. Place the sous vide pouches in the water bath and cook for 2 to 4 hours.

Remove the pouches and place in a ½ ice - ½ water bath until chilled. You can store the pouches in the refrigerator for around 2 days or freeze them for up to 6 months.

Finishing
Preheat a grill to high heat or a pan to medium-high heat.

Put all of the ingredients for the dressing into a food processor and blend until well combined.

Take the chicken out of the sous vide pouches and pat dry. Sear the chicken for 1 to 2 minutes per side, just until browned. Remove from the heat and slice.

Place the lettuce in bowls and top with the pepper, tomato, and mushrooms. Add the dressing, top with the chicken and sunflower seeds, then serve.

SHAVED CHICKEN SANDWICHES

Pre-Bath Time: 15 Minutes
Cooking Time: 2 to 4 Hours
Finishing Time: 30 Minutes
Temperature: 141°F / 60.5°C
Serves: 4

Pre-Bath Ingredients

For the Chicken
4 chicken breasts
½ teaspoon garlic powder
½ teaspoon onion powder
½ teaspoon ancho powder
½ teaspoon dried thyme
Pepper

Finishing Ingredients

For the Onions
2 tablespoons canola or olive oil
1 onion, sliced into ¼" strips
4 cloves garlic, minced
1 red bell pepper, sliced into ¼" strips
½ cup chicken stock
2 tablespoons cider vinegar
Salt and pepper

For the Sandwiches
4 sandwich rolls
4 slices havarti cheese
2 tablespoons thousand island dressing

I love shaved chicken or turkey sandwiches and they come together pretty quickly, especially when you cook the chicken with sous vide. The onion and pepper mixture adds lots of flavor and moisture to them as well.

Pre-Bath

Mix the spices together in a bowl. Pepper the chicken then sprinkle with the spice mixture and seal in a sous vide pouch.

At this point you can store the pouch in the refrigerator for up to 2 days, freeze it for up to 6 months, or cook it right away.

Cooking

Preheat the water bath to 141°F / 60.5°C. Place the sous vide pouches in the water bath and cook for 2 to 4 hours.

Remove the pouches and place in a ½ ice - ½ water bath until chilled. You can store the pouches in the refrigerator for around 2 days or freeze them for up to 6 months.

Finishing

Preheat a water bath to 141°F / 60.5°C. Place the chicken in the water bath until it comes back up to temperature, about 45 minutes.

Preheat the broiler on the oven. Heat a pan to medium heat.

Add the oil to the pan and warm. Add the onion, salt and pepper it, and cook until it begins to soften, about 10 minutes. Add the garlic and bell pepper and cook for another 5 minutes. Add the chicken stock and vinegar and mix well. Cook until it begins to thicken.

Remove the chicken breasts from the water bath and pat dry. Slice them as thin as you can.

Place four piles of the chicken, about the size of the buns, on a roasting sheet. Cover the chicken with the onion and pepper mixture and top with the cheese. Place the rolls on the sheet with the cut side up. Place the roasting sheet under the broiler until the cheese melts and the rolls begin to brown.

Remove the sheet from the oven. Spread the thousand island dressing on the rolls and place the chicken on top of the rolls and serve.

CHICKEN MARSALA

Pre-Bath Time: 5 Minutes
Cooking Time: 2 to 4 Hours
Finishing Time: 30 Minutes
Temperature: 141°F / 60°C
Serves: 4

Pre-Bath Ingredients

4 chicken breasts
1 tablespoon garlic powder
2 thyme sprigs
2 rosemary sprigs
Pepper

Finishing Ingredients

1 cup flour
3 cups sliced mushrooms, such as baby bella,
    crimini, oyster, or porcini
¾ cup Marsala wine
¾ cup chicken stock
3 tablespoons butter
4 tablespoons chopped Italian parsley

*Chicken Marsala is one of my favorite Italian dishes
to make. It is such a simple recipe and is so easy to put
together. Traditionally, the only tricky part is trying
to make sure the chicken breasts are cooked through
without turning them soggy. Using sous vide to pre-
cook the chicken breasts eliminates this issue.*

*Another benefit of using sous vide chicken is that you
can use thicker breasts. Normally, when you make
chicken marsala you pound the chicken into thin filets
¼ of an inch thick to ensure they cook thoroughly. But
here you can use a normal chicken breast or even
butterfly it for one of medium thickness.*

*This dish goes well with a warm baguette and some
angel hair pasta to soak up all the great sauce.
Asparagus or steamed broccoli also is good.*

*Note: If desired, reheat the food in the water bath at
the beginning of the Finishing stage. Otherwise add a
few minutes to the searing time for the middle to
warm.*

Pre-Bath

Pepper the chicken then sprinkle with the
garlic powder. Place in a sous vide pouch
with the thyme and rosemary and seal it.

At this point you can store the pouch in the
refrigerator for up to 2 days, freeze it for up
to 6 months, or cook it right away.

Cooking

Preheat the water bath to 141°F / 60.5°C.
Place the sous vide pouches in the water
bath and cook for 2 to 4 hours.

Remove the pouches and place in a ½ ice - ½
water bath until chilled. You can store the
pouches in the refrigerator for around 2
days or freeze them for up to 6 months.

Finishing

Heat some oil in a saute pan over medium-
high heat.

Remove the sous vide chicken breasts from
the pouch, pat them dry with a paper towel
or dish cloth. Dredge them in the flour and
then quickly sear the chicken breasts for
about 1 minute per side, just enough time to
develop some color. Remove and place
somewhere warm.

Add 1 tablespoon of butter to the pan and
melt. Add the mushrooms to the pan and
cook until they begin to brown and release
their liquid, about 4 to 6 minutes.

Lower the heat to medium and add the
Marsala wine to the pan. Simmer for about 1
minute to cook out the alcohol, scraping the
bottom of the pan to dislodge the browned
bits stuck there. Add the chicken stock to the

pan. Let simmer for 5 to 10 minutes to reduce the sauce.

Put the chicken breasts onto individual plates. Stir the remaining 2 tablespoons of butter into the sauce. Then spoon the mushrooms and marsala sauce evenly over the chicken breasts, top with the Italian parsley and serve.

CHICKEN ENCHILADAS WITH VERDE SAUCE

Pre-Bath Time: 15 Minutes
Cooking Time: 2 to 4 Hours
Finishing Time: 60 Minutes
Temperature: 141°F / 60.5°C
Serves: 4

Pre-Bath Ingredients

1 pound chicken breasts
1 teaspoon garlic powder
1 teaspoon onion powder
¼ teaspoon chipotle chile powder, or chile
    powder of your choice
Pepper

Finishing Ingredients

For the Salsa Verde
4 garlic cloves, halved
½ onion, roughly chopped
2 poblano peppers, deseeded and destemmed
1 jalapeno pepper, deseeded and destemmed
10 tomatillos, destemmed, dehusked, and rinsed
1 tablespoon honey
¼ cup coarsely chopped fresh cilantro

For the Enchiladas
12 small corn tortillas
1 12-ounce can black beans
1 cup cooked corn kernels
½ cup shredded mild cheddar cheese
1½ cups shredded Monterey Jack cheese
2 cups diced tomatoes

These enchiladas are a great way to utilize chicken breasts you have cooked with sous vide. Even though we call for them to be seasoned before cooking this dish is great with unseasoned chicken as well if you have it sitting around. The roasting of the salsa ingredients adds a richness and depth of flavor to the dish. You can add anything to the enchiladas that you want and use more or less cheese and spices, depending on your preferences.

Since you bake the resulting dish we recommend adding the chicken directly to the dish without bringing it back up to temperature.

Pre-Bath

Mix the spices together in a bowl. Pepper the chicken then sprinkle with the spice mixture and seal in a sous vide pouch.

At this point you can store the pouch in the refrigerator for up to 2 days, freeze it for up to 6 months, or cook it right away.

Cooking

Preheat the water bath to 141°F / 60.5°C. Place the sous vide pouches in the water bath and cook for 2 to 4 hours.

Remove the pouches and place in a ½ ice - ½ water bath until chilled. You can store the pouches in the refrigerator for around 2 days or freeze them for up to 6 months.

Finishing

Preheat the broiler on your oven.

Place the garlic, onion, poblanos, jalapeno, and tomatillos on a roasting sheet with raised sides. Salt and pepper them and drizzle with oil. Cook them until they begin to soften and brown, 10 to 15 minutes. Remove the pan from the oven and turn it to 450°F / 232°C. Scrape the roasted veggies and their juices into a food processor or blender. Add the honey and cilantro and process to the consistency you prefer. Salt and pepper to taste.

Remove the chicken from the pouches and cut into ½" strips. Cover the bottom of a baking dish with some of the salsa verde.

Lay out the tortillas and top each one with the chicken, beans, corn, and some cheddar cheese. Roll up the tortillas and place in the baking dish side by side. Top with the remaining salsa verde and the Monterey Jack cheese. Place in the oven and bake until they are bubbly and the cheese is melted, about 10 to 15 minutes. Remove from the heat, top with the diced tomatoes, then serve.

Spicy Duck with Cucumber-Mint Salad

Pre-Bath Time: 15 Minutes
Cooking Time: 2 to 4 Hours
Finishing Time: 45 Minutes
Temperature: 131°F / 55°C
Serves: 4

Pre-Bath Ingredients

For the Duck
2-3 duck breasts, about 2 pounds
2 tablespoons cumin
1 tablespoon ancho chile powder, or chile
    powder of your choice
1 teaspoon chipotle chile powder, or chile
    powder of your choice
Pepper

Finishing Ingredients

For the Salad
1 cucumber, seeded and diced
2 tomatoes, diced
¼ red onion, thinly sliced
¼ cup finely chopped mint leaves
¼ cup unflavored yogurt
1 tablespoon lemon juice
Salt and pepper

The spices on the duck are cooled by the cucumbers and yogurt. The salad also adds a nice crunchy texture to the dish.

This is one of the cases where I really like to sear the food without bringing it back to temperature first. This allows you to really get a great crust on the duck without overcooking it any, especially on the fat side.

Pre-Bath

Mix the spices together in a bowl. Pepper the duck then sprinkle with the half of the spice mixture, reserving the rest for the finishing stage. Place the duck in a sous vide pouch and seal.

At this point you can store the pouch in the refrigerator for up to 2 days, freeze it for up to 6 months, or cook it right away.

Cooking

Preheat the water bath to 131°F / 55°C. Place the sous vide pouches in the water bath and cook for 2 to 4 hours.

Remove the pouches and place in a ½ ice - ½ water bath until chilled. You can store the pouches in the refrigerator for around 2 days or freeze them for up to 6 months.

Finishing

Heat a pan over medium-high heat.

To make the salad, place all of the ingredients into a bowl and mix well.

Remove the duck breasts from the sous vide pouches and pat dry. Score the duck fat in a diamond pattern and sprinkle the entire breast with the remaining spice rub.

When the pan is heated place the duck in it and sear, turning every few minutes until the duck has a nice crust and is heated through.

Remove from the heat and cut into ¼" thick slices. Serve with the cucumber salad on the side.

Duck Sweet Fried Rice

Pre-Bath Time: 15 Minutes
Cooking Time: 2 to 4 Hours
Finishing Time: 45 Minutes
Temperature: 131°F / 55°C
Serves: 4

Pre-Bath Ingredients

For the Duck
2 duck breasts
1 teaspoon ground cinnamon
½ teaspoon cloves
½ teaspoon fennel seeds
½ teaspoon allspice
Pepper

Finishing Ingredients

For the Fried Rice
2 tablespoons canola oil
1 sweet onion, diced
3 carrots, diced
2 cloves garlic, diced
1 jalapeno pepper, diced
1 tablespoon grated fresh ginger
1 egg
2 cups cooked long grain rice
1 cup diced pineapple
½ cup corn kernels, cooked
½ cup peas, cooked
2 tablespoons soy sauce
1 tablespoon rice vinegar

For Garnish
¼ cup chopped fresh parsley

Fried rice is a staple at Chinese restaurants and making it at home is a pretty easy task. Here we pair it with a duck breast flavored with sweet spices and add some pineapple for added flavor. To save time you can make extra rice and freeze it in 1 to 2 cup portions in ziploc bags for later use.

Note: If desired, reheat the food in the water bath at the beginning of the Finishing stage. Otherwise add a few minutes to the searing time for it to warm.

Pre-Bath

Mix the spices together in a bowl. Pepper the duck then sprinkle with the spice mixture and seal in a sous vide pouch.

At this point you can store the pouch in the refrigerator for up to 2 days, freeze it for up to 6 months, or cook it right away.

Cooking

Preheat the water bath to 131°F / 55°C. Place the sous vide pouches in the water bath and cook for 2 to 4 hours.

Remove the pouches and place in a ½ ice - ½ water bath until chilled. You can store the pouches in the refrigerator for around 2 days or freeze them for up to 6 months.

Finishing

Heat two pans over medium-high heat.

Add the oil to one pan and warm. Add the onion and carrots and cook for 5 to 10 minutes until the carrots begin to soften. Add the garlic, jalapeno, and ginger and cook for 1 to 2 minutes. Remove the vegetables from the pan and set aside.

Add the egg to the pan and scramble it for 1 to 2 minutes. Add the rice, pineapple, corn, peas, and the onion mixture to the pan and mix well. Stir in the soy sauce and rice vinegar and cook until heated throughout.

Remove the duck breasts from the sous vide pouches and pat dry. Sear them in the other pan, about 1 to 2 minutes per side. Remove from the heat and cut into ¼" thick slices.

Place a spoonful of the rice in a bowl. Lay several of the strips of duck on top, sprinkle with the parsley, then serve.

LAMB CHOPS WITH SPICY MINT RELISH

Pre-Bath Time: 10 Minutes
Cooking Time: 2 to 4 Hours
Finishing Time: 30 Minutes
Temperature: 131°F / 55°C
Serves: 4

Pre-Bath Ingredients
For the Lamb
8 lamb chops
1 teaspoon dried thyme
1 teaspoon garlic powder
Pepper

Finishing Ingredients
For the Relish
3 tablespoons lime juice
1 cucumber, peeled, seeded, and diced
½ cup diced red onion
1-3 jalapeno chilies, seeded and diced
⅓ cup chopped fresh mint

The relish has a spicy, minty flavor to it that pairs well with the lamb chops. It's very simple to put together and also goes well with chicken or turkey.

Note: If desired, reheat the food in the water bath at the beginning of the Finishing stage. Otherwise add a few minutes to the searing time for the middle to warm.

Pre-Bath
Mix together the spices in a bowl. Pepper the lamb then sprinkle with the spices. Place the lamb chops in the sous vide pouch and seal.

At this point you can store the pouch in the refrigerator for up to 2 days, freeze it for up to 6 months, or cook it right away.

Cooking
Preheat the water bath to 131°F / 55°C. Place the sous vide pouches in the water bath and cook for 2 to 4 hours.

Remove the pouches and place in a ½ ice - ½ water bath until chilled. You can store the pouches in the refrigerator for around 2 days or freeze them for up to 6 months.

Finishing
Preheat a pan over medium-high heat or a grill over high heat.

Up to 30 minutes before the lamb is done make the relish by combining all the ingredients in a large bowl and mixing well.

Take the lamb chops out of the sous vide bath and pat dry. Sear them just until browned, 1 to 2 minutes per side.

Serve the lamb chops with a spoonful or two of the relish on top.

ROGAN JOSH SPICED LAMB LOIN

Pre-Bath Time: 15 Minutes
Cooking Time: 2 to 4 Hours
Finishing Time: 30 Minutes
Temperature: 131°F / 55°C
Serves: 4

Pre-Bath Ingredients
For the Lamb
2-3 pound lamb loin
1 tablespoon garlic powder
2 teaspoons paprika
1 teaspoon ground coriander
½ teaspoon ground cloves
½ teaspoon ground cinnamon
¼ teaspoon ancho chile powder, or chile powder
   of your choice
¼ teaspoon cayenne chile powder, or chile
   powder of your choice
1 bay leaf
Pepper

Finishing Ingredients
For the Herb Salad
½ cup chopped fresh mint
¼ cup chopped fresh dill
1 cup arugula
1 cup frisée lettuce, coarsely chopped
1 tablespoon olive oil
1 lemon
Salt and pepper

Rogan Josh is a classic lamb dish from Kashmir, India. We take the spices normally used in it to create a rub for the lamb loin. The herbs in this salad help to add some brightness to counteract the richness and flavor of the Rogan Josh spiced loin.

Note: If desired, reheat the food in the water bath at the beginning of the Finishing stage. Otherwise add a few minutes to the searing time for the middle to warm.

Pre-Bath
Mix together the spices in a bowl. Pepper the lamb then sprinkle with the spices. Place the lamb in the sous vide pouch with the bay leaf and seal.

At this point you can store the pouch in the refrigerator for up to 2 days, freeze it for up to 6 months, or cook it right away.

Cooking
Preheat the water bath to 131°F / 55°C. Place the sous vide pouches in the water bath and cook for 2 to 4 hours.

Remove the pouches and place in a ½ ice - ½ water bath until chilled. You can store the pouches in the refrigerator for around 2 days or freeze them for up to 6 months.

Finishing
Preheat a pan over medium-high heat or a grill to high heat.

Take the lamb out of the sous vide bath and pat dry. Sear it just until browned, 1 to 2 minutes per side. Remove from the heat and cut into ¼" to ½" slices.

Place the slices of lamb on plates and top with the herbs, arugula, and frisée. Sprinkle with salt and pepper. Drizzle the olive oil over top and squeeze the lemon equally over the portions.

PASTA WITH SAUSAGE AND SUMMER SQUASH

Pre-Bath Time: 10 Minutes
Cooking Time: 2 to 3 Hours
Finishing Time: 30 Minutes
Temperature: 135°F / 57.2°C
Serves: 4

Pre-Bath Ingredients
1 pound sweet Italian sausage
1 teaspoon ground sage

Finishing Ingredients
12 ounces farfalle pasta, or pasta or your choice
1 yellow onion, cut into ¼" slices
1 zucchini, cut into ½" wide half-moons
1 yellow squash, cut into ½" wide half-moons
4 cloves garlic, diced
½ cup chicken stock
1 tablespoon lemon juice
2 tablespoons basil

I love pasta with a nice, earthy sauce and sweet Italian sausage. The sausage is first sous vided to ensure it is perfectly cooked then it is chilled. On the day you want to eat you simply sear the sausages to crisp up the outside and warm the middle. Then make a quick vegetable stir fry to go on top of the pasta. It comes together pretty fast and is really tasty.

I recommend using the sausage straight from the refrigerator so you can really firm up the casings.

Pre-Bath
Sprinkle the sausage links with the sage then seal in a sous vide pouch.

At this point you can store the pouch in the refrigerator for up to 2 days, freeze it for up to 6 months, or cook it right away.

Cooking
Preheat the water bath to 135°F / 57.2°C. Place the sous vide pouches in the water bath and cook for 2 to 3 hours.

Remove the pouches and place in a ½ ice - ½ water bath until chilled. You can store the pouches in the refrigerator for around 2 days or freeze them for up to 6 months.

Finishing
Preheat a pan to medium-high heat. Bring a pot of salted water to a boil.

Add the farfalle to the water and cook until tender.

Take the sausages out of the pouches and pat dry. Sear them in the pan until browned on all sides, 1 to 2 minutes per side. Remove from the heat and slice into ½" rounds.

Add the onion to the pan and cook until it begins to turn translucent, about 5 minutes. Add the zucchini and yellow squash to the pan along with the garlic and cook until the squash begins to soften.

Add the chicken stock, lemon juice, sausage rounds, and pasta to the pan cook until the sauce reduces slightly and coats the vegetables. Remove from the heat and serve with the basil sprinkled on top.

BRATWURST GRINDERS

Pre-Bath Time: 10 Minutes
Cooking Time: 2 to 3 Hours
Finishing Time: 30 Minutes
Temperature: 135°F / 57.2°C
Serves: 4

Pre-Bath Ingredients
4 large bratwurst links

Finishing Ingredients
Olive oil
4 hoagie or sub rolls, cut to hold the sausage
Good mustard
8 slices provolone cheese
¼ sweet onion, diced
Relish

These brats are a great meal to have during the week when you want something filling from the grill without spending too much time making it. I recommend using the brats straight from the refrigerator so you can firm up the casings. You can substitute any toppings that you prefer.

Pre-Bath
Seal the sausage links in a sous vide pouch.

At this point you can store the pouch in the refrigerator for up to 2 days, freeze it for up to 6 months, or cook it right away.

Cooking
Preheat the water bath to 135°F / 57.2°C. Place the sous vide pouches in the water bath and cook for 2 to 3 hours.

Remove the pouches and place in a ½ ice - ½ water bath until chilled. You can store the pouches in the refrigerator for around 2 days or freeze them for up to 6 months.

Finishing
Heat a grill to high heat.

Brush olive oil on the cut side of the hoagie rolls. Place the rolls cut side down on the grill and cook until they start to brown. Remove from the heat and smear each side with the mustard and places 2 slices of cheese on each one.

Remove the bratwurst from their pouches and pat them dry. Sear them on the grill, turning as the casing cooks, until nicely browned and warmed throughout.

Remove from the heat and place on the grilled hoagie rolls. Top with the diced onion and relish and serve.

ASIAN GLAZED PORK CHOPS

Pre-Bath Time: 15 Minutes
Cooking Time: 3 to 6 Hours
Finishing Time: 30 Minutes
Temperature: 135°F / 57.5°C
Serves: 4

Pre-Bath Ingredients
For the Pork Chops
4 pork chops
1 tablespoon Chinese 5-spice powder
Pepper

Finishing Ingredients
For the Glaze
½ cup hoisin sauce
¼ cup rice vinegar
¼ cup soy sauce
1 tablespoon sesame oil
1 tablespoon lime juice
1 tablespoon honey
2 teaspoons minced ginger
2 cloves garlic, minced

For the Garnish
¼ cup chopped fresh cilantro
1 teaspoon sesame seeds

These Asian pork chops have a sweet and salty hoisin glaze on them that really ups the flavor of sometimes bland pork chops. I recommend cooking them on the grill but you can also cook them under the broiler in your oven.

I usually sear the pork chops when they are just out of the refrigerator or at room temperature. This allows me more time to really develop the glaze. I make sure to remove them from the heat once the center is warm, about 115°F / 46°C, but you can do it straight from the water bath, just reduce the amount of time it is seared.

Pre-Bath
Pepper the pork chops then, sprinkle with the Chinese 5-spice powder. Place in the sous vide pouches and seal.

At this point you can store the pouch in the refrigerator for up to 2 days, freeze it for up to 6 months, or cook it right away.

Cooking
Preheat the water bath to 135°F / 57.2°C. Place the sous vide pouches in the water bath and cook for 3 to 6 hours.

Remove the pouches and place in a ½ ice - ½ water bath until chilled. You can store the pouches in the refrigerator for around 2 days or freeze them for up to 6 months.

Finishing
Preheat a grill to high heat.

To prepare the glaze mix together all of the ingredients in a bowl until combined well.

Take the pork out of the pouches and pat dry. Sear them on the grill until grill marks form, a couple minutes per side. Once they brown brush the glaze on each and turn once the sauce begins to caramelize, about 30-45 seconds. Repeat several times until they are coated with the glaze and the center of the chops has raised to around 115°F / 46°C.

Remove from the heat and serve with the cilantro and sesame seeds on top.

Bourbon Glazed Pork Tenderloin

Pre-Bath Time: 15 Minutes
Cooking Time: 3 to 6 Hours
Finishing Time: 45 Minutes
Temperature: 135°F / 57.5°C
Serves: 4

Pre-Bath Ingredients
For the Pork
1-2 pounds pork tenderloin
1 teaspoon dried sage
1 teaspoon allspice
½ teaspoon ginger
Pepper

Finishing Ingredients
For the Glaze
1 cup bourbon whiskey
½ cup brown sugar
½ cup ketchup
2 teaspoons Worcester sauce
1 teaspoon liquid smoke
¼ cup apple juice
1 tablespoon lemon juice
1 teaspoon minced garlic
½ teaspoon cayenne pepper
¼ teaspoon dry mustard
Salt and pepper

This simple recipe takes a sometimes bland pork tenderloin and adds layers of flavor with the glaze. I usually sear the pork when it is just out of the refrigerator or at room temperature. This allows me more time to develop the glaze on it.

To save time you can also skip the step of reducing the sauce and just use it after you combine all the ingredients but the flavors will not be as strong.

Pre-Bath
Mix the spices together in a bowl. Pepper the pork tenderloin, sprinkle with the spices, then place in the sous vide pouches and seal.

At this point you can store the pouch in the refrigerator for up to 2 days, freeze it for up to 6 months, or cook it right away.

Cooking
Preheat the water bath to 135°F / 57.2°C. Place the sous vide pouches in the water bath and cook for 3 to 6 hours.

Remove the pouches and place in a ½ ice - ½ water bath until chilled. You can store the pouches in the refrigerator for around 2 days or freeze them for up to 6 months.

Finishing
Preheat a grill to high heat or the broiler in the oven.

To prepare the glaze mix together all of the ingredients in a pot over medium-high heat and bring to a simmer, stirring occasionally. Cook for about 30 minutes, until it thickens some.

Take the pork out of the pouches and pat dry. Sear on the grill until grill marks form on the first side, a couple of minutes. Brush the glaze on the side facing up and turn the tenderloin. Repeat several times until it is coated with the glaze, cooking about 30 to 60 seconds per turn.

Remove from the heat, brush once more with the glaze, slice into ½" rounds and serve.

SPICY TURKEY BREAST WITH AVOCADO SALAD

Pre-Bath Time: 15 Minutes
Cooking Time: 2 to 4 Hours
Finishing Time: 30 Minutes
Temperature: 141°F / 60.5°C
Serves: 4

Pre-Bath Ingredients

For the Turkey
1-2 pounds turkey breasts or filets
1 teaspoon garlic powder
1 teaspoon chipotle chile powder or chile
    powder of your choice
1 teaspoon paprika
Pepper

Finishing Ingredients

For the Vinaigrette
2 tablespoons lemon juice
1 garlic clove, minced
⅓ cup olive oil
Salt and pepper

For the Salad
7 cups arugula or baby spinach
1 avocado, sliced
Parmigiano-Reggiano Cheese, for shaving

*I really enjoy turkey for a light dinner and it goes well
with this avocado and arugula salad from Beginning
Sous Vide. Here we add some spice to the turkey in
the form of chipotle powder. It's a great way to kick up
the heat and flavor without overpowering the turkey.*

*Note: If desired, reheat the food in the water bath at
the beginning of the Finishing stage. Otherwise add a
few minutes to the searing time for the middle to
warm.*

Pre-Bath

Mix together the spices in a bowl. Pepper
the turkey then sprinkle with the spices.
Place in the sous vide pouch and seal.

At this point you can store the pouch in the
refrigerator for up to 2 days, freeze it for up
to 6 months, or cook it right away.

Cooking

Preheat the water bath to 141°F / 60.5°C.
Place the sous vide pouches in the water
bath and cook for 2 to 4 hours.

Remove the pouches and place in a ½ ice - ½
water bath until chilled. You can store the
pouches in the refrigerator for around 2
days or freeze them for up to 6 months.

Finishing

First make the vinaigrette. Combine the
lemon juice and garlic in a bowl, add some
salt and pepper and let sit for a few minutes.
Slowly whisk in the olive oil until the
mixture thickens.

Take the turkey out of the sous vide pouches
and pat dry. Sear for 1 to 2 minutes per side,
just until browned. Remove from the heat
and cut into strips.

Place the arugula in a serving bowl and add
enough vinaigrette to flavor it, tossing to
mix. Top the arugula with the avocado slices
and chicken. Spoon a bit more dressing over
them and season with salt and pepper.
Using a vegetable peeler, shave strips of
Parmesan cheese over the top and serve.

GREEN CURRY WITH TURKEY

Pre-Bath Time: 15 Minutes
Cooking Time: 2 to 4 Hours
Finishing Time: 30 Minutes
Temperature: 141°F / 60.5°C
Serves: 4

Pre-Bath Ingredients

For the Turkey
1 pound turkey breasts or cutlets, cut into 1"
    chunks
1 tablespoon garlic powder
1 teaspoon onion powder
1 teaspoon ginger powder
Pepper

Finishing Ingredients

For the Curry
1 tablespoon oil
1 onion, chopped
2 carrots, peeled and cut into ¼" rounds
2 garlic cloves, minced
1 teaspoon ground cumin
2 tablespoons green curry paste
1½ cups coconut milk
½ cup water
½ cup green beans, cut into short pieces
1 tablespoon fish sauce
1½ tablespoons lime juice
1 tablespoon honey
¼ cup cilantro leaves

*I always enjoy the flavor of green curry and this
recipe is a very easy way to make it at home. You can
always add more curry paste if you want a hotter
curry, or even a diced jalapeno. I usually serve this
with rice or bread to soak up all the liquid.*

Pre-Bath

Mix together the spices in a bowl. Pepper
the turkey then sprinkle with the spices.
Place in the sous vide pouch and seal.

At this point you can store the pouch in the
refrigerator for up to 2 days, freeze it for up
to 6 months, or cook it right away.

Cooking

Preheat the water bath to 141°F / 60.5°C.
Place the sous vide pouches in the water
bath and cook for 2 to 4 hours.

Remove the pouches and place in a ½ ice - ½
water bath until chilled. You can store the
pouches in the refrigerator for around 2
days or freeze them for up to 6 months.

Finishing

Preheat a water bath to 141°F / 60.5°C. Place
the turkey in the water bath until it comes
back up to temperature, about 30 to 45
minutes.

Heat a pan over medium heat. Add the oil
and warm. Add the onion, carrots, garlic,
and cumin and cook until the onion softens
and takes on some color. Add the curry
paste and stir constantly for about 1 minute.
Add the coconut milk and water and bring
to a boil. Add the beans then turn down the
heat and simmer for 10 minutes.

Just before serving stir in the fish sauce, lime
juice, and honey.

Take the turkey out of the pouches and place
in individual bowls. Pour the curry over the
top and garnish with the cilantro leaves.

QUICK SIDES

Side dishes can be a great way to add variety to your menu without having to learn all new meals. Many of the sides below go with multiple meals and can be used in a variety of ways.

Tips and Tricks

Break Out the Rice

Some of the quickest and best tasting sides are rice dishes. They are very easy to put together and most cook within 10 to 45 minutes, about how long it will take to finish many of the meals in this book.

It's also easy to add lots of flavor to rice. When you are making it substitute half of the water for chicken stock for a richer, deeper flavor. You can also saute onions, peppers (mild or hot), carrots, and/or garlic in the pot before adding the rice and liquid. For a sweeter rice try adding a tablespoon of sugar and at the end add raisins, pistachios, or chopped-up dates. Many herbs like basil, parsley, oregano, and cilantro can also be added at the end of the cooking time to impart a nice herby flavor to the rice, or woodier herbs like thyme and rosemary can be added at the beginning of the cooking process.

Pasta Bulks Up Any Meal

Pasta cooks fast and it can add depth to any meal. Depending on the sauce it can complement a mild white fish or stand up to a flavorful roast.

Light sauces are also easy to add to pasta and can introduce new flavors. Many pastas are great when tossed with good olive oil, lemon juice, and some freshly grated parmigiano-reggiano cheese as soon as you take them out of the water. You can also

make (or buy) pesto and toss the pasta with it for an herby and very flavorful dish.

For heartier sauces you can quickly make a carbonara sauce by adding lots of parmesan cheese and a raw egg to the pasta as soon as it comes off the heat and stir them together, as the egg cooks it forms a creamy sauce. You can also use leftover, or bottled, tomato sauces that you can warm up and add to the pasta.

Whichever method you choose, pasta is a great complement to many dishes, especially when you are short on time and want something on the table quick. They also have the benefit of being another hands-off cooking technique.

Go Seasonal

One easy way to create side dishes is to cook seasonally with fresh, local ingredients. Fresh vegetables have such great flavor that it is hard for dishes using them to come out poorly. Especially during summer you can utilize fresh tomatoes, cucumbers, corn, beans, and squash in many different ways.

Simple Salsas are Great

If you are cooking a normal weekday meal then a quick and easy way to finish off sous vided meat is to just add a simple salsa to the top of it. This is especially easy in summer. Simply chop up some fresh vegetables like tomatoes, corn, avocado or squash, add some herbs like basil or oregano and toss together with some olive oil and a splash of apple cider or red wine vinegar. Plate the salsa on the seared meat and you are all done. And the dish even looks fancy!

OTHER SIDES IN THIS BOOK

There are many side dishes that are called for in the other recipes in this book. Here is a list of them for easy reference.

LEMON ASPARAGUS

Total Preparation Time: 10 to 15 Minutes
Serves: 2 as a side

Ingredients
1 bunch asparagus, ends cut off
1 lemon
Good olive oil for drizzling
Parmesan cheese for grating
Salt and pepper

Asparagus is a very simple side to fix when you are in a hurry. Once you blanch them in salted, boiling water you can add any number of seasonings to make it compliment the meal you are having. Here we go very simple and just add some lemon for acidity and Parmesan for umani or savoriness.

This side comes together very quickly so it should be made as your main course is being finished. The asparagus only cooks for 5 to 10 minutes and then is ready.

Zest the outside of the lemon then cut the lemon in half.

Bring a pot of salted water to a boil. Add the asparagus and cook until it becomes tender, 5 to 10 minutes depending on the thickness of the asparagus.

Drain the asparagus and place on the plates. Top with some of the lemon zest and fresh ground pepper. Drizzle with olive oil and squeeze some lemon juice on top. Finally, shave some Parmesan cheese on the top using a microplane or grater and serve.

SAVORY ASPARAGUS WITH PANCETTA

Total Preparation Time: 15 to 20 Minutes
Serves: 2 as a side

Ingredients
1 bunch asparagus, ends cut off
1 cup diced pancetta
1 tablespoon fresh thyme
¼ cup chicken stock
Salt and pepper

We take the asparagus in a different direction here and pair it with pancetta and chicken stock for richness and add fresh thyme for some herby notes. You can substitute bacon if you don't have pancetta.

Note: I always recommend using homemade chicken stock since it's easy to make and tastes much better than store bought stock.

Bring a pot of salted water to a boil. Add the asparagus and cook until it becomes tender, 5 to 10 minutes depending on the thickness of the asparagus.

Heat a pan over medium heat and add the pancetta. Cook until the fat is rendered and the pancetta begins to turn crispy.

Drain the asparagus and pat dry with a paper towel or kitchen cloth. Add to the pan with the pancetta along with the fresh thyme and chicken stock. Cook until the chicken stock reduces slightly and begins to stick to the asparagus, 2 to 5 minutes.

Remove from the heat and serve.

Broccoli Raab With Hot Peppers and Garlic

Total Preparation Time: 30 Minutes
Serves: 4 to 6 as a side

Ingredients
2 tablespoons olive oil
1 bunch broccoli raab, trimmed and cleaned
4 cloves garlic, diced
½ teaspoon hot pepper flakes
Salt and pepper

Broccoli raab is a classic Italian side dish and it is very simple to put together. It goes great with most pastas and is also wonderful when served with a steak or roast, or even duck breast. Feel free to adjust the amount of pepper flakes to make it as hot as you'd like.

Heat a pan over medium heat.

Add the oil to the pan and warm. Add the broccoli raab, garlic, and pepper flakes and cook for a few minutes.

Add 1 tablespoon of water to the pan, lower the heat and cook until tender. Salt and pepper to taste then serve.

Sesame Broccoli

Total Preparation Time: 30 Minutes
Serves: 4 to 6 as a side

Ingredients
2 tablespoons peanut oil
1 large broccoli, cut into bite sized pieces
3 cloves garlic, minced
½ cup chicken stock
1 tablespoon soy sauce
1 tablespoon sesame oil
2 tablespoons oyster sauce
1 tablespoon sesame seeds
1 tablespoon cold water
1 tablespoon corn starch
Salt and pepper

Broccoli gets a bad rap for being a plain or tasteless dish. Here's a great way to add a lot of flavor to it while still keeping it very healthy. It goes great with chicken or turkey and you can even double the ingredients for the sauce and use it on the protein as well.

Heat a pan over medium-high heat. Add the oil and warm. Add the broccoli and cook for a few minutes, until just beginning to brown.

Add the garlic, chicken stock, soy sauce, sesame oil, and oyster sauce then stir to combine well. Turn the heat to medium, cover and cook until the broccoli is tender, 3 to 5 minutes. Salt and pepper to taste.

Mix together the cold water and corn starch. Gradually whisk it into the sauce until it thickens and clings to the broccoli.

Remove from the heat, top with the sesame seeds and serve.

CARAMELIZED CARROTS

Total Preparation Time: 30 Minutes
Serves: 4 to 6 as a side

Ingredients

2 tablespoons peanut oil
12 carrots, peeled and cut into ½" disks
2 tablespoons butter
1 teaspoon white sugar
2 sprigs fresh rosemary
2 tablespoons chopped fresh parsley
Salt and pepper

Caramelized carrots are a great addition to many meals and add a sweetness and hardiness. They are often served with beef or lamb roasts but also go well with chicken.

Heat a pan over medium heat.

Add the oil to the pan and warm. Add the carrots and cook, stirring often, until they begin to brown on all sides. Add the butter, sugar, and rosemary and cook until the carrots are nice and tender. Salt and pepper to taste.

Remove the carrots from the heat, sprinkle with the fresh parsley and serve.

SPICY CARROT SALAD

Total Preparation Time: 30 Minutes
Serves: 4 to 6 as a side

Ingredients

1 tablespoon lemon juice
2 tablespoons red wine vinegar
2 cloves garlic, minced
½ cup olive oil
6 carrots, peeled and julienned or grated
1 jalapeno, deseeded and diced
1 tablespoon chopped fresh tarragon
1 tablespoon chopped fresh parsley
Salt and pepper

This is a nice salad that adds a bit of heat and crunch to meals. It is great served on the side or even as a topping for a rich steak. You could even use it as a garnish on pulled pork sandwiches.

First make the dressing. In a large bowl mix together the lemon juice, vinegar, and garlic. Slowly whisk in the olive oil.

Add the carrots, jalapeno and herbs and mix well. Salt and pepper to taste and serve.

Cucumber and Watermelon Salad

Total Preparation Time: 20 Minutes
Serves: 4 to 6 as a side

Ingredients
3 tablespoons fresh lime juice
2 tablespoons red wine vinegar
½ tablespoon brown sugar
3 cups cubed watermelon, seeded
2 cups cubed cucumber
1 jalapeno chile, seeded, minced
¼ cup chopped fresh mint
Salt and pepper

Cucumber and watermelon go together really well. We add some sugar, vinegar, lime juice, and mint for seasoning and to help the cucumber and watermelon shine. Taste the watermelon before making the dressing and depending on how sweet it is you can adjust the amount of brown sugar you add.

Make the dressing by whisking together the lime juice, red wine vinegar, and sugar.

In a bowl combine the watermelon, cucumber, and jalapeno chile. Pour the dressing over the top and mix to combine.

Salt and pepper to taste and garnish with the mint when serving.

Fennel Salad

Total Preparation Time: 20 Minutes
Serves: 4 to 6 as a side

Ingredients
1 tablespoon fresh lemon juice
3 tablespoons fresh orange juice
½ cup olive oil
Salt and pepper
3 fennel bulbs, cored and thinly sliced
½ red onion, thinly sliced
10 cherry tomatoes, halved
¼ cup blue cheese or gorgonzola cheese

This simple side dish is great with fish, especially salmon or sea bass. It can also be used to balance out a heavier meat like steak or a roast. If you are not using the fennel fronds for anything else you can use them as garnish to top the salad.

Make the dressing by whisking together the lemon juice, orange juice, and olive oil.

Pile the fennel and onion slices on a plate and add the tomatoes and blue cheese. Drizzle the dressing on top and serve.

SMOKY GREEN BEANS WITH TOMATOES

Total Preparation Time: 20 Minutes
Serves: 4 as a side

Ingredients
2 strips bacon, diced
1 onion, thinly sliced
3 cloves garlic, diced
1 pound fresh green beans, trimmed and cleaned
1 14.5 ` diced tomatoes
Salt and pepper
2 tablespoons chopped fresh basil

Green beans are a fast and nutritious side dish. We combine them with Smoky bacon and diced tomatoes to boost the flavor. If you have time in summer using fresh tomatoes is a wonderful way to add more flavor.

Heat a pan over medium-high heat.

Add the bacon and cook until the fat is rendered. Discard all but 1 tablespoon of the bacon fat. Add the onion and garlic then cook until they soften, about 5 minutes. Add the beans and cook for a few minutes then add the canned tomatoes, along with their juices and mix well. Let simmer for several minutes until the beans are tender.

Season with salt and pepper, remove from the heat and serve with the basil on top.

GREEN BEANS WITH SLICED ALMONDS

Total Preparation Time: 20 Minutes
Serves: 4 as a side

Ingredients
½ cup sliced almonds
2 tablespoons olive oil
1 pound fresh green beans, trimmed and cleaned
½ cup chicken stock
1 teaspoon lemon juice
Salt and pepper
1 tablespoon lemon zest

These beans are very easy to put together and come out with a rich flavor from the chicken stock. If you prefer vegetarian beans you can replace the chicken stock with vegetable broth or simply water.

Heat a pan over medium-high heat.

Add the almonds to the pan without oil in it and cook until they just begin to brown and turn fragrant, 1 or 2 minutes. Remove the almonds and set aside.

Add the olive oil to the pan and warm. Add the green beans and cook for several minutes until they just begin to take on color or start to become tender. Add the chicken stock and lemon juice and mix well. Cook until the beans are tender and the stock clings to them.

Season with salt and pepper, remove from the heat and serve with the lemon zest and almonds on top.

MUSHROOMS WITH BRANDY-CREAM SAUCE

Total Preparation Time: 20 Minutes
Serves: 4 as a side

Ingredients
¼ cup olive oil
20-30 baby bella or white button mushrooms,
    thickly sliced
1 teaspoon fresh thyme
3 cloves garlic, chopped
¼ teaspoon cayenne pepper, or chile powder of
    your choice
¼ cup brandy
¼ cup heavy cream
1 teaspoon lemon juice
1 tablespoon chopped fresh parsley
Salt and pepper

*These mushrooms are rich and decadent. They can
hold their own next to a flavorful steak or roast.*

Heat a pan over medium heat. Add the olive oil and let it warm. Add the mushrooms and cook until they begin to brown, about 5 minutes. Add the thyme, garlic, and cayenne pepper and mix together.

Remove the pan from the stove. Add the brandy. Move the pan back to the stove, being careful not to ignite any brandy fumes and cook until it reduces, 2 or 3 minutes. Add the heavy cream and lemon juice and stir to combine. Reduce to a nice consistency and until the mushrooms are cooked through, another 3 to 5 minutes.

Salt and pepper to taste then remove from the heat, sprinkle with the parsley, and serve.

GARLIC SAUTEED MUSHROOMS

Total Preparation Time: 20 Minutes
Serves: 4 as a side

Ingredients
16 ounces mushrooms, cleaned and cut to size
3 tablespoons butter
4 cloves garlic, minced
½ teaspoon fresh thyme
Salt and pepper

*I love mushrooms sauteed with garlic. They have such
a rich, deep flavor to them with a nice bite from the
garlic. These are great served with steak or chicken
and can stand up to most heavy dishes.*

Heat a pan over medium heat.

Add the butter to the pan and let it melt. Add the garlic and let it cook for about 1 minute. Add the mushrooms and thyme and cook until the mushrooms begin to brown, about 5 minutes. Stir the mushrooms and continue cooking until they are tender.

SMOKY PEAS

Total Preparation Time: 10 to 15 Minutes
Serves: 2 as a side

Ingredients
4 strips bacon, cut into ¼" batons
2 cloves garlic, minced
2 cups frozen peas
1 teaspoon paprika
2 teaspoons white wine vinegar
Salt and pepper

These peas come together really fast and add a lot of flavor to a dish. The bacon and paprika add a smoky taste and for more smoke with some heat you could add some chipotle chile powder.

Heat a pan over medium heat. Add the bacon strips and cook until the fat is rendered and they begin to get crispy, about 7 minutes.

Add the garlic and cook for 1 minute. Then add the peas, paprika, and vinegar and cook until the peas are heated through. Salt and pepper to taste then remove from the heat and serve.

ROASTED FINGERLING POTATO SALAD

Total Preparation Time: 30 to 45 Minutes
Serves: 4 as a side

3 pounds small fingerling potatoes, cleaned and halved or quartered
Olive oil
1 tablespoon fresh thyme
6 garlic cloves, diced
¼ cup olive oil
2 tablespoons apple cider vinegar
2 tablespoons Dijon mustard
3 shallots, diced
Salt and pepper

4 tablespoons chopped fresh parsley
2 tablespoons chopped fresh tarragon

This salad uses a tangy Dijon mustard dressing and garlic to flavor the fingerling potatoes. It's great as a side for most grilled meats and many sandwiches.

Pre-heat your oven to 400°F / 204°C.

Place the potatoes on a baking sheet with raised sides. Drizzle with the olive oil and sprinkle with the thyme. Mix well and spread out into an even layer.

Place in the oven until the potatoes start to brown, about 20 minutes. Add the garlic and stir the potatoes, trying to get the tops and bottoms reversed. Cook until they become tender, about 10 minutes more.

Remove the potatoes from the oven and place in a large bowl.

In a separate container whisk together the olive oil, vinegar, mustard, and shallots. Pour it on top of the potatoes and mix well. Sprinkle the parsley and tarragon on top and serve.

Radish, Strawberry and Spinach Salad

Total Preparation Time: 20 Minutes
Serves: 4 as a side

Ingredients

For the Dressing
⅓ cup fresh orange juice
2 teaspoons honey
1 teaspoon Dijon mustard
6 tablespoons olive oil

For the Salad
6 cups baby spinach, washed and dried
3 radishes, thinly sliced
½ yellow bell pepper, diced
12 strawberries, sliced
2 tablespoons sunflower seeds
¼ cup crumbled blue cheese

Fresh strawberries strike a nice balance between sweet and tart. We showcase them in this salad along with radishes and bell peppers. We top it off with a orange vinaigrette for some added tang.

First make the dressing by whisking together all of the dressing ingredients in a small bowl.

Place the spinach in bowls and add the radishes, bell pepper and strawberries. Drizzle with the dressing then top with the sunflower seeds and blue cheese. Sprinkle with some salt and freshly cracked pepper.

Roasted Root Vegetables

Total Preparation Time: 45 to 60 Minutes
Serves: 4 as a side

Ingredients
1 potato, cut into 1" cubes
2-3 turnips, cut into 1" cubes
4 large carrots, cut into 1" rounds
6 garlic cloves, quartered
1 tablespoon fresh thyme
1 tablespoon chopped fresh rosemary
2-3 tablespoons olive oil
Salt and pepper

These roasted root vegetables are a great way to add substance to a dish. They go well with beef, chicken, or pork roasts. You can use any root vegetables you have on hand.

Preheat the oven to 400°F / 204°C.

Place the vegetables on a sheet pan with raised sides. Sprinkle the garlic, thyme, and rosemary on top. Drizzle the olive oil over everything and pepper the vegetables. Toss everything to mix well and spread out into an even layer.

Place in the oven until the vegetables start to brown, about 20 minutes. Stir the vegetables, trying to get the tops and bottoms reversed. Cook until they become tender, another 10 to 20 minutes.

Remove from the heat and serve.

SAUTEED SNAP PEAS

Total Preparation Time: 10 Minutes
Serves: 2 as a side

Ingredients
1 tablespoon olive oil
1 pound snap peas or snow peas, cleaned
1 tablespoon butter
1 tablespoon fresh lemon juice
1 tablespoon mint
Salt and pepper

Snap and snow peas are great in spring when they are fresh off the plants. Here we cook them about as simply as you can with some olive oil and a squeeze of lemon juice. You can also add sliced carrots to this dish to help round out a meal.

Heat a pan over medium heat.

Add the oil to the pan and warm. Add the snap peas and cook, stirring often, until they become tender. Add the butter and lemon juice and mix well. Salt and pepper to taste.

Remove the peas from the heat, sprinkle with the mint and serve.

GLAZED SNAP PEAS

Total Preparation Time: 20 Minutes
Serves: 2 as a side

Ingredients
1 pound snap peas or snow peas, cleaned
½ cup chicken stock
1 teaspoon thyme
3 tablespoons butter
Salt and pepper

Here we kick up the flavor of the peas by cooking them in chicken stock and adding thyme. This stands up better to heavy dishes and won't be overwhelmed by bold flavors.

Heat a pan over medium heat. Add the peas, chicken stock, and thyme. Cook, stirring frequently, until the stock has been absorbed and clings to the peas. Stir in the butter and cook until the peas become nice and tender. Remove from the heat and serve.

GRILLED SUMMER SQUASH

Total Preparation Time: 20 Minutes
Serves: 4 as a side

Ingredients
2-3 summer squash, cut lengthwise in ½" planks
Olive oil
1 tablespoon garlic powder
1 teaspoon paprika
Salt and pepper

My favorite way to prepare summer squash is by seasoning them lightly and then grilling them until just tender. This works great with zucchini, yellow crookneck, and patty pan squash. Feel free to change around the seasonings as you see fit.

Heat a grill to medium-high or high heat.

Drizzle the zucchini slices with the olive oil, then sprinkle with the garlic powder and paprika then salt and pepper them.

Cook them on the grill for 5 to 10 minutes, flipping once or twice, until they start to become tender.

Remove from the heat and serve.

BAKED SUMMER SQUASH

Total Preparation Time: 60 Minutes
Serves: 4 as a side

Ingredients
2-3 summer squash, sliced into ⅛" rounds, preferably using the small setting of a mandolin
1 sweet onion, thinly sliced
Olive oil
5 cloves garlic, minced
3 tablespoons fresh thyme leaves
1 14.5-ounce can diced tomatoes
1 cup grated fresh Parmesan cheese
Salt and pepper

Even though the cooking of this dish takes some time the actual prep work isn't very hard, especially if you have a mandolin. You can also add mozzarella cheese if you like it even cheesier.

Heat the oven to 400°F / 204°C.

In a roasting pan lay down a layer of squash as if you were making lasagna. Add a layer of onion slices, garlic, thyme leaves, and tomatoes. Repeat until the pan is full.

Top with the parmesan cheese and bake until the cheese is browned and the squash is tender, about 30 to 40 minutes. Remove from the heat and serve.

Time and Temperature Charts

You can also get this time and temperature information
on your mobile phone if you have an iPhone, iPad or an Android.

Just search for "Sous Vide" and look for the guide by "Primolicious".

One of the most interesting aspects of sous vide cooking is how much the time and temperature used can change the texture of the food. Many people experiment with different cooking times and temperatures to tweak dishes various ways.

The numbers below are merely beginning recommendations and are a good place to start. Feel free to increase or lower the temperature several degrees or play around with the cooking time as you see fit as long as you stay in the safe-zone.

DONENESS RANGE

One of the most common questions we get asked about our sous vide recipes is some variation of "the recipe says to cook it for 3 to 6 hours, but when is it actually done".

The short answer is that anytime within the given range the food is "done". As long as the food has been in the water bath for more than the minimum time and less than the maximum time, then it is done. There isn't a specific magical moment of true doneness that can be generalized.

For those that want more information, here's the explanation why.

The How and Why

To have this conversation we first need to determine what "done" actually means. For sous vide there are two main "doneness" concerns when cooking your food. The first is to ensure that the food actually comes up to the temperature you are cooking it at (or becomes pasteurized at for some food). The second concern is making sure the food is tender enough to eat without being "over tender", mushy, or dry.

Once the food you are cooking is completely up to temperature and it is tenderized enough to eat (and not over tenderized), it is now "done". For some already tender cuts of meat like filets, loins, and chicken breasts you don't have to worry about tenderness since they start out that way. That means that these cuts are "done" once they get up to temperature. You can find out this time using our Sous Vide Thickness Ruler.

However, despite them being "done" at the minimum time shown, they stay "done" for several hours past that time, depending on the starting tenderness of the meat. This is why we give a range. You can eat a 1" cut of filet mignon after 50 minutes but you can also eat the filet up to 3 hours after it has gone into the bath without any loss in quality, tenderness, or flavor.

This is how our ranges are determined. They specify that for an average cut of the given meat, they will become "great to eat" tender at the minimum time given. They will continue to get more tender the longer they are in the bath but will remain "great to eat" tender until the final time given, at which point they may begin to get mushy and overcooked. In essence, they will be "done", and very tasty, for that entire span between the minimum and maximum times.

Another Way to Look at It

Another way to think about how this works is to use the following analogy. Pretend you were helping a new cook grill a steak. If they told you they wanted to cook it medium rare and asked you to tell them how to tell when it was "done", what would you say?

Most people would reply with "when the temperature is between 131°F to 139°F".

If the friend isn't a cook they would ask "Yeah, but when is it actually done?"

The answer at this point really comes down to personal preference since to some people medium rare is perfect at 131°F and others prefer a little more well-done 135°F, but a medium rare steak is "done" anywhere in that range.

Other Critical Variables

One other complicating factor is that there are many variables that go into determining how fast a piece of meat tenderizes and/or becomes tender.

The most obvious variable is that some cuts of meat are tougher than others. For example, a top round roast needs to be tenderized a lot longer than a ribeye. Most people realize this and that's why almost all sous vide charts break the food down by "cut".

Another less obvious but almost as important factor is where the meat came from. There is a big difference between how fast the meat tenderizes and how the cow was raised. I've found that grass-fed meat from my local farmer needs just 1/2 the time to become tender compared to supermarket meat (this is also true when roasting or braising them). I've also talked to a reader in Mexico who eats local grass-fed beef that needs slightly longer times than normal because the cows work more.

There are then the variables in the actual cow itself. Whether the meat is prime, choice, etc. makes a difference in tenderizing time. As does the marbling, how old the meat is, and several other factors.

So taking all of this together it can be hard to accurately determine a range of "doneness" that will work for all cuts of meat. But we try our best to come up with a nice range of times that the "average" piece of meat will be done in. The only way to really learn is to experiment with the types of meat in your area and see how they react. And luckily for us, sous vide allows us to have a wide range that food is done in.

In Conclusion

So while there might be one magical moment in the cooking process where a certain piece of meat is the most ideal tenderness, in practice there is a wide time range in the cooking process where the meat will be "done". As long as you take it out sometime in that range it should turn out great.

As you get more experience with your local meats, and determine your personal preferences, you can start to tweak your cook times to suit them more exactly. But as you are learning just remember that the food will be "done" anywhere in that range, and don't sweat the details!

BEEF ROASTS AND TOUGH CUTS

Bottom Round Roast

Medium Rare	131°F for 2 to 3 Days (55.0°C)
Medium	140°F for 2 to 3 Days (60.0°C)
Well-Traditional	160°F for 1 to 2 Days (71.1°C)

Brisket

Medium Rare	131°F for 2 to 3 Days (55.0°C)
Medium	140°F for 2 to 3 Days (60.0°C)
Well-Traditional	160°F for 1 to 2 Days (71.1°C)

Cheek

Medium Rare	131°F for 2 to 3 Days (55.0°C)
Medium	149°F for 2 to 3 Days (65.0°C)
Well-Traditional	160°F for 1 to 2 Days (71.1°C)

Chuck Roast

Medium Rare	131°F for 2 to 3 Days (55.0°C)
Medium	140°F for 2 to 3 Days (60.0°C)
Well-Traditional	160°F for 1 to 2 Days (71.1°C)

Pot Roast

Medium Rare	131°F for 2 to 3 Days (55.0°C)
Medium	140°F for 2 to 3 Days (60.0°C)
Well-Traditional	160°F for 1 to 2 Days (71.1°C)

Prime Rib Roast

Medium Rare	131°F for 5 to 10 Hours (55°C)
Medium	140°F for 5 to 10 Hours (60°C)

Rib Eye Roast

Medium Rare	131°F for 5 to 10 Hours (55°C)
Medium	140°F for 5 to 10 Hours (60°C)

Ribs

Medium Rare	131°F for 2 to 3 Days (55.0°C)
Medium	140°F for 2 to 3 Days (60.0°C)
Well-Traditional	160°F for 1 to 2 Days (71.1°C)

Shank

Medium Rare	131°F for 2 to 3 Days (55.0°C)
Medium	140°F for 2 to 3 Days (60.0°C)
Well-Traditional	160°F for 1 to 2 Days (71.1°C)

Short Ribs

Medium Rare	131°F for 2 to 3 Days (55.0°C)
Medium	140°F for 2 to 3 Days (60.0°C)
Well-Traditional	160°F for 1 to 2 Days (71.1°C)

Sirloin Roast

Medium Rare	131°F for 5 to 10 Hours (55.0°C)
Medium	140°F for 5 to 10 Hours (60.0°C)

Stew Meat

Medium Rare	131°F for 4 to 8 Hours (55.0°C)
Medium	140°F for 4 to 8 Hours (60.0°C)

Sweetbreads

Medium	140°F for 30 to 45 Min (60°C)
Pre-Roasting	152°F for 60 Min (66.7°C)

Tenderloin Roast

Medium Rare	131°F for 3 to 6 Hours (55.0°C)
Medium	140°F for 3 to 6 Hours (60.0°C)

Tongue

Low and Slow	140°F for 48 Hours (60.0°C)
High and Fast	158°F for 24 Hours (70.0°C)

Top Loin Strip Roast

Medium Rare	131°F for 4 to 8 Hours (55.0°C)
Medium	140°F for 4 to 8 Hours (60.0°C)

Top Round Roast

Medium Rare	131°F for 1 to 3 Days (55.0°C)
Medium	140°F for 1 to 3 Days (60.0°C)
Well-Traditional	160°F for 1 to 2 Days (71.1°C)

Tri-Tip Roast

Medium Rare	131°F for 5 to 10 Hours (55°C)
Medium	140°F for 5 to 10 Hours (60°C)

Beef - Steak and Tender Cuts

Blade Steak
Medium Rare	131°F for 4 to 10 Hours (55.0°C)
Medium	140°F for 4 to 10 Hours (60.0°C)

Bottom Round Steak
Medium Rare	131°F for 1 to 3 Days (55.0°C)
Medium	140°F for 1 to 3 Days (60.0°C)

Chuck Steak
Medium Rare	131°F for 1 to 2 Days (55.0°C)
Medium	140°F for 1 to 2 Days (60.0°C)

Eye Round Steak
Medium Rare	131°F for 1 to 2 Days (55.0°C)
Medium	140°F for 1 to 2 Days (60.0°C)

Flank Steak
Medium Rare	131°F for 2 to 12 Hours (55.0°C)
Medium Rare and Tender	131°F for 1 to 2 Days (55.0°C)
Medium	140°F for 2 to 12 Hours (60.0°C)
Medium and Tender	140°F for 1 to 2 Days (60.0°C)

Flat Iron Steak
Medium Rare	131°F for 4 to 10 Hours (55.0°C)
Medium	140°F for 4 to 10 Hours (60.0°C)

Hamburger
Medium Rare	131°F for 2 to 4 Hours (55.0°C)
Medium	140°F for 2 to 4 Hours (60.0°C)

Hanger Steak
Medium Rare	131°F for 2 to 3 Hours (55.0°C)
Medium	140°F for 2 to 3 Hours (60.0°C)

Porterhouse Steak
Medium Rare	131°F for 2 to 3 Hours (55.0°C)
Medium	140°F for 2 to 3 Hours (60.0°C)

Rib Steak
Medium Rare	131°F for 2 to 8 Hours (55.0°C)
Medium	140°F for 2 to 8 Hours (60.0°C)

Ribeye Steak
Medium Rare	131°F for 2 to 8 Hours (55.0°C)
Medium	140°F for 2 to 8 Hours (60.0°C)

Sausage
Medium Rare	131°F for 2 to 3 Hours (55.0°C)
Medium	140°F for 90 to 120 Min (60°C)

Shoulder Steak
Medium Rare	131°F for 4 to 10 Hours (55.0°C)
Medium	140°F for 4 to 10 Hours (60.0°C)

Sirloin Steak
Medium Rare	131°F for 2 to 10 Hours (55.0°C)
Medium	140°F for 2 to 10 Hours (60.0°C)

Skirt Steak
Medium Rare	131°F for 1 to 2 Days (55.0°C)
Medium	140°F for 1 to 2 Days (60.0°C)

T-Bone Steak
Medium Rare	131°F for 2 to 3 Hours (55.0°C)
Medium	140°F for 2 to 3 Hours (60.0°C)

Tenderloin Steak
Medium Rare	131°F for 2 to 3 Hours (55.0°C)
Medium	140°F for 2 to 3 Hours (60.0°C)

Top Loin Strip Steak
Medium Rare	131°F for 2 to 3 Hours (55.0°C)
Medium	140°F for 2 to 3 Hours (60.0°C)

Top Round Steak
Medium Rare	131°F for 1 to 2 Days (55.0°C)
Medium	140°F for 1 to 2 Days (60.0°C)

Tri-Tip Steak
Medium Rare	131°F for 2 to 10 Hours (55.0°C)
Medium	140°F for 2 to 10 Hours (60.0°C)

CHICKEN AND EGGS

Breast

Rare	136°F for 1 to 4 Hours (57.8°C)
Medium / Typical	140°F - 147°F for 1 to 4 Hours (63.9°C)
More Dry	140°F - 147°F for 4 to 12 Hours (63.9°C)

Drumstick

Rare	140°F for 90 to 120 Min (60.0°C)
Ideal	148°F - 156°F for 2 to 5 Hours (64.4°C)
For Shredding	160°F - 170°F for 8 to 12 Hours (71.1°C)

Eggs

Over Easy	142°F - 146°F for 45 to 60 Min (62.8°C)
Poached	142°F for 45 to 60 Min (61.1°C)
Perfect	148°F for 45 to 60 Min (64.4°C)
Hard Boiled	149°F - 152°F for 45 to 60 Min (65.6°C)
Pasteurized	135°F for 75 Min (57.2°C)

Leg

Rare	140°F for 90 to 120 Min (60.0°C)
Ideal	148°F - 156°F for 2 to 5 Hours (64.4°C)
For Shredding	160°F - 170°F for 8 to 12 Hours (71.1°C)

Sausage

White Meat	140°F for 1 to 2 Hours (63.9°C)
Mixed Meat	140°F for 90 to 120 Min (60.0°C)

Thigh

Rare	140°F for 90 to 120 Min (60.0°C)
Ideal	148°F - 156°F for 2 to 5 Hours (64.4°C)
For Shredding	160°F - 170°F for 8 to 12 Hours (71.1°C)

Whole Chicken

Rare	140°F for 4 to 6 Hours (60.0°C)
Typical	148°F for 4 to 6 Hours (64.4°C)
Larger	148°F for 6 to 8 Hours (64.4°C)
Butterflied	148°F for 2 to 4 Hours (64.4°C)

DUCK

Breast

Medium Rare	131°F for 2 to 4 Hours (55.0°C)
Medium	140°F for 2 to 4 Hours (60.0°C)

Drumstick

Medium Rare	131°F for 3 to 6 Hours (55.0°C)
Well	176°F for 8 to 10 Hours (80.0°C)
Confit	167°F for 10 to 20 Hours (75.0°C)

Foie Gras

Foie Gras	134°F for 35 to 55 Min (56.7°C)

Leg

Medium Rare	131°F for 3 to 6 Hours (55.0°C)
Well	176°F for 8 to 10 Hours (80.0°C)
Duck Confit	167°F for 10 to 20 Hours (75.0°C)

Sausage

Breast Meat	131°F for 1 to 2 Hours (55.0°C)
Mixed Meat	131°F for 2 to 3 Hours (55.0°C)

Thigh

Medium Rare	131°F for 3 to 6 Hours (55.0°C)
Well	176°F for 8 to 10 Hours (80.0°C)
Confit	167°F for 10 to 20 Hours (75.0°C)

Whole Duck

Medium Rare	131°F for 3 to 6 Hours (55.0°C)
Medium	140°F for 3 to 6 Hours (60.0°C)
Confit	167°F for 10 to 20 Hours (75.0°C)

FISH AND SHELLFISH

Arctic Char
"Sushi", Rare	104°F for 10 to 30 Min (40.0°C)
"Sushi", Medium Rare	122°F for 10 to 30 Min (50.0°C)
Medium Rare	132°F for 10 to 30 Min (55.6°C)
Medium	140°F for 10 to 30 Min (60.0°C)

Bass
"Sushi", Rare	104°F for 10 to 30 Min (40.0°C)
"Sushi", Medium Rare	122°F for 10 to 30 Min (50.0°C)
Medium Rare	132°F for 10 to 30 Min (55.6°C)
Medium	140°F for 10 to 30 Min (60.0°C)

Black Sea Bass
"Sushi", Rare	104°F for 10 to 30 Min (40.0°C)
"Sushi", Medium Rare	122°F for 10 to 30 Min (50.0°C)
Medium Rare	132°F for 10 to 30 Min (55.6°C)
Medium	140°F for 10 to 30 Min (60.0°C)

Bluefish
"Sushi", Medium Rare	122°F for 10 to 30 Min (50.0°C)
Medium Rare	132°F for 10 to 30 Min (55.6°C)
Medium	140°F for 10 to 30 Min (60.0°C)

Carp
"Sushi", Medium Rare	122°F for 10 to 30 Min (50.0°C)
Medium Rare	132°F for 10 to 30 Min (55.6°C)
Medium	140°F for 10 to 30 Min (60.0°C)

Catfish
"Sushi", Medium Rare	122°F for 10 to 30 Min (50.0°C)
Medium Rare	132°F for 10 to 30 Min (55.6°C)
Medium	140°F for 10 to 30 Min (60.0°C)

Cod
Rare	104°F for 10 to 30 Min (40.0°C)
"Sushi", Medium Rare	129°F for 10 to 30 Min (53.9°C)
Medium Rare	132°F for 10 to 30 Min (55.6°C)

Flounder
"Sushi", Medium Rare	122°F for 10 to 30 Min (50.0°C)
Medium Rare	132°F for 10 to 30 Min (55.6°C)
Medium	140°F for 10 to 30 Min (60.0°C)

Grouper
"Sushi", Rare	104°F for 10 to 30 Min (40.0°C)
"Sushi", Medium Rare	122°F for 10 to 30 Min (50.0°C)
Medium Rare	132°F for 10 to 30 Min (55.6°C)
Medium	140°F for 10 to 30 Min (60.0°C)

Haddock
"Sushi", Medium Rare	122°F for 10 to 30 Min (50.0°C)
Medium Rare	132°F for 10 to 30 Min (55.6°C)
Medium	140°F for 10 to 30 Min (60.0°C)

Hake
"Sushi", Rare	104°F for 10 to 30 Min (40.0°C)
"Sushi", Medium Rare	122°F for 10 to 30 Min (50.0°C)
Medium Rare	132°F for 10 to 30 Min (55.6°C)
Medium	140°F for 10 to 30 Min (60.0°C)

Halibut
"Sushi", Rare	104°F for 10 to 30 Min (40.0°C)
"Sushi", Medium Rare	129°F for 10 to 30 Min (53.9°C)
Medium Rare	132°F for 10 to 30 Min (55.6°C)
Medium	140°F for 10 to 30 Min (60.0°C)

King Crab Tail
King Crab Tail	140°F for 30 to 45 Min (60.0°C)

Lobster
Medium Rare	126°F for 15 to 40 Min (52.2°C)
Medium	140°F for 15 to 40 Min (60.0°C)

Mackerel
"Sushi", Rare	109°F for 10 to 30 Min (42.8°C)
"Sushi", Medium Rare	122°F for 10 to 30 Min (50.0°C)
Medium Rare	132°F for 10 to 30 Min (55.6°C)

Mahi Mahi

"Sushi", Medium Rare	122°F for 10 to 30 Min (50.0°C)
Medium Rare	132°F for 10 to 30 Min (55.6°C)
Medium	140°F for 10 to 30 Min (60.0°C)

Marlin

"Sushi", Rare	104°F for 10 to 30 Min (40.0°C)
"Sushi", Medium Rare	122°F for 10 to 30 Min (50.0°C)
Medium Rare	132°F for 10 to 30 Min (55.6°C)
Medium	140°F for 10 to 30 Min (60.0°C)

Monkfish

"Sushi", Rare	104°F for 10 to 30 Min (40.0°C)
"Sushi", Medium Rare	118°F for 10 to 30 Min (47.8°C)
Medium Rare	132°F for 10 to 30 Min (55.6°C)
Medium	140°F for 10 to 30 Min (60.0°C)

Octopus

Slow Cook	170°F for 4 to 7 Hours (76.7°C)
Fast Cook	180°F for 2 to 3 Hours (82.2°C)

Red Snapper

"Sushi", Rare	104°F for 10 to 30 Min (40.0°C)
"Sushi", Medium Rare	122°F for 10 to 30 Min (50.0°C)
Medium Rare	132°F for 10 to 30 Min (55.6°C)
Medium	140°F for 10 to 30 Min (60.0°C)

Salmon

"Sushi", Rare	104°F for 10 to 30 Min (40.0°C)
"Sushi", Medium Rare	122°F for 10 to 30 Min (50.0°C)
Medium Rare	132°F for 10 to 30 Min (55.6°C)
Medium	140°F for 10 to 30 Min (60.0°C)

Sardines

"Sushi", Rare	104°F for 10 to 30 Min (40.0°C)
"Sushi", Medium Rare	122°F for 10 to 30 Min (50.0°C)
Medium Rare	132°F for 10 to 30 Min (55.6°C)
Medium	140°F for 10 to 30 Min (60.0°C)

Scallops

Pre-Sear	122°F for 15 to 35 Min (50.0°C)

Scrod

"Sushi", Medium Rare	122°F for 10 to 30 Min (50.0°C)
Medium Rare	132°F for 10 to 30 Min (55.6°C)
Medium	140°F for 10 to 30 Min (60.0°C)

Sea Bass

"Sushi", Rare	104°F for 10 to 30 Min (40.0°C)
"Sushi", Medium Rare	122°F for 10 to 30 Min (50.0°C)
Medium Rare	132°F for 10 to 30 Min (55.6°C)
Medium	140°F for 10 to 30 Min (60.0°C)

Shark

"Sushi", Medium Rare	122°F for 10 to 30 Min (50.0°C)
Medium Rare	132°F for 10 to 30 Min (55.6°C)
Medium	140°F for 10 to 30 Min (60.0°C)

Shrimp

"Sushi" Medium Rare	122°F for 15 to 35 Min (50.0°C)
Medium Rare	132°F for 15 to 35 Min (55.6°C)

Skate

"Sushi", Medium Rare	129°F for 10 to 30 Min (53.9°C)
Medium Rare	132°F for 10 to 30 Min (55.6°C)
Medium	140°F for 10 to 30 Min (60.0°C)

Soft Shell Crab

Standard	145°F for 3 hours (62.8°C)

Sole

"Sushi", Medium Rare	122°F for 10 to 30 Min (50.0°C)
Medium Rare	132°F for 10 to 30 Min (55.6°C)
Medium	143°F for 10 to 30 Min (61.7°C)

Squid

Pre-Sear	113°F for 45 to 60 Min (45.0°C)
Low Heat	138°F for 2 to 4 Hours (58.9°C)
High Heat	180°F for 1 Hour (82.2°C)

Striped Bass
"Sushi", Rare	104°F for 10 to 30 Min (40.0°C)
"Sushi", Medium Rare	122°F for 10 to 30 Min (50.0°C)
Medium Rare	132°F for 10 to 30 Min (55.6°C)
Medium	140°F for 10 to 30 Min (60.0°C)

Sturgeon
"Sushi", Rare	104°F for 10 to 30 Min (40.0°C)
"Sushi", Medium Rare	122°F for 10 to 30 Min (50.0°C)
Medium Rare	132°F for 10 to 30 Min (55.6°C)
Medium	140°F for 10 to 30 Min (60.0°C)

Swordfish
"Sushi", Rare	104°F for 10 to 30 Min (40.0°C)
"Sushi", Medium Rare	122°F for 10 to 30 Min (50.0°C)
Medium Rare	132°F for 10 to 30 Min (55.6°C)
Medium	140°F for 10 to 30 Min (60.0°C)

Tilapia
"Sushi", Rare	104°F for 10 to 30 Min (40.0°C)
"Sushi", Medium Rare	122°F for 10 to 30 Min (50.0°C)
Medium Rare	132°F for 10 to 30 Min (55.6°C)
Medium	140°F for 10 to 30 Min (60.0°C)

Trout
"Sushi", Medium Rare	122°F for 10 to 30 Min (50.0°C)
Medium Rare	132°F for 10 to 30 Min (55.6°C)
Medium	140°F for 10 to 30 Min (60.0°C)

Tuna
"Sushi", Rare	100°F for 10 to 20 Min (37.8°C)
"Sushi", Medium Rare	129°F for 10 to 30 Min (53.9°C)
Medium Rare	132°F for 10 to 30 Min (55.6°C)

Turbot
"Sushi", Medium Rare	129°F for 10 to 30 Min (53.9°C)
Medium Rare	132°F for 10 to 30 Min (55.6°C)
Medium	140°F for 10 to 30 Min (60.0°C)

FRUITS AND VEGETABLES

Acorn Squash	183°F for 1 to 2 Hours (83.9°C)	**Pears**	183°F for 25 to 35 Min (83.9°C)
Apples	183°F for 25 to 40 Min (83.9°C)	**Pineapple**	167°F for 45 to 60 Min (75.0°C)
Artichokes	183°F for 45 to 75 Min (83.9°C)	**Plums**	167°F for 15 to 20 Min (75.0°C)
Asparagus	183°F for 30 to 40 Min (83.9°C)	**Potatoes**	
Banana	183°F for 10 to 15 Min (83.9°C)	Small	183°F for 30 to 60 Min (83.9°C)
Beet	183°F for 30 to 60 Min (83.9°C)	Large	183°F for 60 to 120 Min (83.9°C)
Broccoli	183°F for 20 to 30 Min (83.9°C)	**Pumpkin**	183°F for 45 to 60 Min (83.9°C)
Brussels Sprouts	183°F for 45 to 60 Min (83.9°C)	**Radish**	183°F for 10 to 25 Min (83.9°C)
Butternut Squash	183°F for 1 to 2 Hours (83.9°C)	**Rhubarb**	141°F for 25 to 45 Min (60.6°C)
Cabbage	183°F for 30 to 45 Min (83.9°C)	**Rutabaga**	183°F for 2 Hours (83.9°C)
Carrot	183°F for 40 to 60 Min (83.9°C)	**Salsify**	183°F for 45 to 60 Min (83.9°C)
Cauliflower		**Squash, Summer**	183°F for 30 to 60 Min (83.9°C)
Florets	183°F for 20 to 30 Min (83.9°C)	**Squash, Winter**	183°F for 1 to 2 Hours (83.9°C)
For Puree	183°F for 2 Hours (83.9°C)	**Sunchokes**	183°F for 40 to 60 Min (83.9°C)
Stems	183°F for 60 to 75 Min (83.9°C)	**Sweet Potatoes**	
Celery Root	183°F for 60 to 75 Min (83.9°C)	Small	183°F for 45 to 60 Min (83.9°C)
Chard	183°F for 60 to 75 Min (83.9°C)	Large	183°F for 60 to 90 Min (83.9°C)
Cherries	183°F for 15 to 25 Min (83.9°C)	**Swiss Chard**	183°F for 60 to 75 Min (83.9°C)
Corn	183°F for 30 to 45 Min (83.9°C)	**Turnip**	183°F for 30 to 45 Min (83.9°C)
Eggplant	183°F for 30 to 45 Min (83.9°C)	**Yams**	183°F for 30 to 60 Min (83.9°C)
Fennel	183°F for 40 to 60 Min (83.9°C)	**Zucchini**	183°F for 30 to 60 Min (83.9°C)
Golden Beets	183°F for 30 to 60 Min (83.9°C)		
Green Beans	183°F for 30 to 45 Min (83.9°C)		
Leek	183°F for 30 to 60 Min (83.9°C)		
Onion	183°F for 35 to 45 Min (83.9°C)		
Parsnip	183°F for 30 to 60 Min (83.9°C)		
Pea Pods	183°F for 30 to 40 Min (83.9°C)		
Peaches	183°F for 30 to 60 Min (83.9°C)		

LAMB

Arm Chop
Medium Rare	131°F for 18 to 36 Hours (55.0°C)
Medium	140°F for 18 to 36 Hours (60.0°C)

Blade Chop
Medium Rare	131°F for 18 to 36 Hours (55.0°C)
Medium	140°F for 18 to 36 Hours (60.0°C)

Breast
Medium Rare	131°F for 20 to 28 Hours (55.0°C)
Medium	140°F for 20 to 28 Hours (60.0°C)
Well-Traditional	165°F for 20 to 28 Hours (73.9°C)

Leg, Bone In
Rare	126°F for 1 to 2 Days (52.2°C)
Medium Rare	131°F for 2 to 3 Days (55.0°C)
Medium	140°F for 1 to 3 Days (60.0°C)

Leg, Boneless
Medium Rare	131°F for 18 to 36 Hours (55.0°C)
Medium	140°F for 18 to 36 Hours (60.0°C)

Loin Chops
Rare	126°F for 1 to 2 Hours (52.2°C)
Medium Rare	131°F for 2 to 4 Hours (55.0°C)
Medium	140°F for 2 to 3 Hours (60.0°C)

Loin Roast
Rare	126°F for 1 to 2 Hours (52.2°C)
Medium Rare	131°F for 2 to 4 Hours (55.0°C)
Medium	140°F for 2 to 3 Hours (60.0°C)

Loin, Boneless
Rare	126°F for 1 to 2 Hours (52.2°C)
Medium Rare	131°F for 2 to 4 Hours (55.0°C)
Medium	140°F for 2 to 3 Hours (60.0°C)

Neck
Medium Rare	131°F for 2 to 3 Days (55.0°C)
Medium	140°F for 2 to 3 Days (60.0°C)
Well-Traditional	165°F for 1 to 2 Days (73.9°C)

Osso Buco
Medium Rare	131°F for 1 to 2 Days (55.0°C)
Medium	140°F for 1 to 2 Days (60.0°C)
Well-Traditional	165°F for 1 to 2 Days (73.9°C)

Rack
Rare	126°F for 1 to 2 Hours (52.2°C)
Medium Rare	131°F for 2 to 3 Hours (55.0°C)
Medium	140°F for 1 to 3 Hours (60.0°C)

Rib Chop
Rare	126°F for 1 to 2 Hours (52.2°C)
Medium Rare	131°F for 2 to 3 Hours (55.0°C)
Medium	140°F for 1 to 3 Hours (60.0°C)

Ribs
Medium Rare	131°F for 22 to 26 Hours (55.0°C)
Medium	140°F for 22 to 26 Hours (60.0°C)
Well-Traditional	165°F for 22 to 26 Hours (73.9°C)

Shank
Medium Rare	131°F for 1 to 2 Days (55.0°C)
Medium	140°F for 1 to 2 Days (60.0°C)
Well-Traditional	165°F for 1 to 2 Days (73.9°C)

Shoulder
Medium Rare	131°F for 1 to 2 Days (55.0°C)
Medium	140°F for 1 to 2 Days (60.0°C)
Well-Traditional	165°F for 18 to 36 Hours (73.9°C)

Tenderloin
Rare	126°F for 1 to 2 Hours (52.2°C)
Medium Rare	131°F for 2 to 3 Hours (55.0°C)
Medium	140°F for 1 to 3 Hours (60.0°C)

PORK

Arm Steak
Medium Rare   131°F for 1 to 2 Days (55.0°C)
Medium   140°F for 1 to 2 Days (60.0°C)

Baby Back Ribs
Medium Rare   131°F for 8 to 10 Hours (55.0°C)
Medium   140°F for 8 to 10 Hours (60.0°C)
Well-Traditional 155°F for 12 to 24 Hours (68.3°C)

Back Ribs
Medium Rare   131°F for 8 to 12 Hours (55.0°C)
Medium   140°F for 8 to 12 Hours (60.0°C)
Well-Traditional 155°F for 12 to 24 Hours (68.3°C)

Belly
Low and Slow   140°F for 2 to 3 Days (60.0°C)
In Between   160°F for 18 to 36 Hours (71.1°C)
High and Fast   180°F for 12 to 18 Hours (82.2°C)

Blade Chops
Medium Rare   131°F for 8 to 12 Hours (55.0°C)
Medium   140°F for 8 to 12 Hours (60.0°C)

Blade Roast
Medium Rare   131°F for 1 to 2 Days (55.0°C)
Medium   140°F for 1 to 2 Days (60.0°C)
Well-Traditional 155°F for 1 to 2 Days (68.3°C)

Blade Steak
Medium Rare   131°F for 18 to 36 Hours (55.0°C)
Medium   140°F for 18 to 36 Hours (60.0°C)

Boston Butt
Medium Rare   131°F for 1 to 2 Days (55.0°C)
Medium   140°F for 1 to 2 Days (60.0°C)
Well-Traditional 155°F for 1 to 2 Days (68.3°C)

Butt Roast
Medium Rare   131°F for 18 to 36 Hours (55.0°C)
Medium   140°F for 18 to 36 Hours (60.0°C)
Well-Traditional 155°F for 18 to 36 Hours (68.3°C)

Country Style Ribs
Medium Rare   131°F for 8 to 12 Hours (55.0°C)
Medium   140°F for 8 to 12 Hours (60.0°C)
Well-Traditional 155°F for 12 to 24 Hours (68.3°C)

Fresh Side Pork
Low and Slow   140°F for 2 to 3 Days (60.0°C)
In Between   160°F for 18 to 36 Hours (71.1°C)
High and Fast   180°F for 12 to 18 Hours (82.2°C)

Ground Pork
Medium Rare   131°F for 2 to 4 Hours (55.0°C)
Medium   140°F for 2 to 4 Hours (60.0°C)

Ham Roast
Medium Rare   131°F for 10 to 20 Hours (55.0°C)
Medium   140°F for 10 to 20 Hours (60.0°C)
Well-Traditional 155°F for 10 to 20 Hours (68.3°C)

Ham Steak
Medium Rare   131°F for 2 to 3 Hours (55.0°C)
Medium   140°F for 2 to 3 Hours (60.0°C)

Kebabs
Medium Rare   131°F for 3 to 8 Hours (55.0°C)
Medium   140°F for 3 to 8 Hours (60.0°C)
Well-Traditional 155°F for 3 to 8 Hours (68.3°C)

Leg (Fresh Ham)
Medium Rare   131°F for 10 to 20 Hours (55.0°C)
Medium   140°F for 10 to 20 Hours (60.0°C)
Well-Traditional 155°F for 10 to 20 Hours (68.3°C)

Loin Chop
Medium Rare   131°F for 3 to 5 Hours (55.0°C)
Medium   140°F for 2 to 4 Hours (60.0°C)

Loin Roast
Medium Rare   131°F for 4 to 8 Hours (55.0°C)
Medium   140°F for 4 to 6 Hours (60.0°C)

Picnic Roast
Medium Rare   131°F for 1 to 3 Days (55.0°C)
Medium   140°F for 1 to 3 Days (60.0°C)
Well-Traditional 155°F for 1 to 3 Days (68.3°C)

Pork Chops
Medium Rare   131°F for 3 to 6 Hours (55.0°C)
Medium   140°F for 2 to 4 Hours (60.0°C)

Rib Chops

Medium Rare	131°F for 5 to 8 Hours (55.0°C)
Medium	140°F for 4 to 7 Hours (60.0°C)

Rib Roast

Medium Rare	131°F for 5 to 8 Hours (55.0°C)
Medium	140°F for 4 to 7 Hours (60.0°C)

Sausage

Medium Rare	131°F for 2 to 3 Hours (55.0°C)
Medium	140°F for 2 to 3 Hours (60.0°C)
Well-Traditional	155°F for 2 to 3 Hours (68.3°C)

Shank

Medium Rare	131°F for 8 to 10 Hours (55.0°C)
Medium	140°F for 8 to 10 Hours (60.0°C)

Shoulder

Medium Rare	135°F for 1 to 2 Days (57.2°C)
Medium	145°F for 1 to 2 Days (62.8°C)
Well-Traditional	155°F for 1 to 2 Days (68.3°C)

Sirloin Chops

Medium Rare	131°F for 6 to 12 Hours (55.0°C)
Medium	140°F for 5 to 10 Hours (60.0°C)

Sirloin Roast

Medium Rare	131°F for 6 to 12 Hours (55.0°C)
Medium	140°F for 5 to 10 Hours (60.0°C)
Well-Traditional	155°F for 10 to 16 Hours (68.3°C)

Spare Ribs

Medium Rare	131°F for 12 to 24 Hours (55.0°C)
Medium	140°F for 12 to 24 Hours (60.0°C)
Well-Traditional	155°F for 12 to 24 Hours (68.3°C)

Spleen

Spleen	145°F for 1 Hour (62.8°C)

Tenderloin

Medium Rare	131°F for 3 to 6 Hours (55.0°C)
Medium	140°F for 2 to 4 Hours (60.0°C)

TURKEY

Breast
"Rare"   136°F for 1 to 4 Hours (57.8°C)
Medium / Typical   140°F - 147°F for 1 to 4 Hours (63.9°C)

Drumstick
Medium Rare   140°F for 3 to 4 Hours (60.0°C)
Ideal   148°F for 4 to 8 Hours (64.4°C)
For Shredding   160°F for 18 to 24 Hours (71.1°C)

Leg
Medium Rare   140°F for 3 to 4 Hours (60.0°C)
Ideal   148°F for 4 to 8 Hours (64.4°C)
For Shredding   160°F for 18 to 24 Hours (71.1°C)

Sausage
White Meat   140°F for 1 to 4 Hours (63.9°C)
Mixed Meat   140°F for 3 to 4 Hours (64.4°C)

Thigh
Medium Rare   140°F for 3 to 4 Hours (60.0°C)
Ideal   148°F for 4 to 8 Hours (64.4°C)
For Shredding   160°F for 18 to 24 Hours (71.1°C)

FAHRENHEIT TO CELSIUS CONVERSION

This guide gives temperatures in both Fahrenheit and Celsius but to convert from Fahrenheit to Celsius take the temperature, then subtract 32 from it and multiply the result by 5/9:

(Fahrenheit - 32) * 5/9 = Celsius

We've listed out the temperatures from 37°C to 87°C which are the most commonly used range in sous vide.

Celsius	Fahrenheit	Celsius	Fahrenheit
37	98.6	64	147.2
38	100.4	65	149.0
39	102.2	66	150.8
40	104.0	67	152.6
41	105.8	68	154.4
42	107.6	69	156.2
43	109.4	70	158.0
44	111.2	71	159.8
45	113.0	72	161.6
46	114.8	73	163.4
47	116.6	74	165.2
48	118.4	75	167.0
49	120.2	76	168.8
50	122.0	77	170.6
51	123.8	78	172.4
52	125.6	79	174.2
53	127.4	80	176.0
54	129.2	81	177.8
55	131.0	82	179.6
56	132.8	83	181.4
57	134.6	84	183.2
58	136.4	85	185.0
59	138.2	86	186.8
60	140.0	87	188.6
61	141.8	88	190.4
62	143.6	89	192.2
63	145.4	90	194.0

COOKING BY THICKNESS

For more Cooking by thickness information you can view our equipment section on our website where we have an iPhone thickness ruler and free printable thickness cards.

You can find them on our website here:
http://bit.ly/e7Lth2

There are two ways to cook sous vide, one is based on the thickness of the food and the other is based on the desired tenderness.

Cooking based on thickness is how PolyScience, Baldwin, and Nathan started out as they did research on food safety. Cooking sous vide based on thickness basically tells you the minimum time you can cook a piece of meat to ensure it is safe and comes up to temperature in the middle. It doesn't take into account tenderizing time or any other factors. It's often used by restaurants or home cooks who want to minimize cooking time and are using tender cuts of meat that don't need the tenderization.

Cooking sous vide based on tenderness takes into account how tough a piece of meat is and how long it needs to be cooked in order to make it appealing. So a chuck steak needs to be cooked a lot longer than a filet, even though they are both safe after the same amount of time. As long as the minimum cooking time is met for the temperature used, then it's completely safe to eat.

Both sous vide methods have their uses. Thickness-based is great for very tender cuts cooked by people who need them done in the minimum amount of time. Tenderness-based is best for tougher cuts or people that have a range of time that they are interested in.

A Few Notes on the Times

Times were extrapolated from the descriptions in Baldwin's Practical Guide to Sous Vide (http://bit.ly/hGOtjd) and Sous Vide for the Home Cook, as well as Nathan's tables on eGullet and a few other sources. (http://bit.ly/eVHjS3).

The times are also approximate since there are many factors that go into how quickly food is heated. The density of the food matters a lot, which is one reason beef heats differently than chicken. To a lesser degree where you get your beef from will affect the cooking time, and whether the beef was factory raised, farm raised, or grass-fed. Because of this, I normally don't try to pull it out at the exact minute it is done unless I'm in a rush.

The times shown are also minimum times and food can be, and sometimes needs to be, left in for longer periods in order to fully tenderize the meat. If you are cooking food longer, remember that food should not be cooked at temperatures less than 131°F (55°C) for more than 4 hours.

BEEF, PORK, LAMB THICKNESS CHART

Heat from Refrigerator to Any Temperature

How long it will take to heat an entire piece of meat from 41°F / 5°C to the temperature of the water bath.

Reminder, this food might not be pasteurized at these times and food should not be cooked at temperatures less than 131°F / 55°C for more than 4 hours.

While there are slight differences in the heating time for different temperatures of water baths, the times usually vary less than 5 to 10% even going from a 111°F / 44°C bath to a 141°F / 60.5°C bath, which equates to a difference of 5 minutes every hour. We show the largest value in our chart, so if you are cooking it at a lower temperature you can knock a little of the time off.

Heat from Freezer to Any Temperature

How long it will take to heat an entire piece of meat from 32°F / -18°C to the temperature of the water bath.

Reminder, this food might not be pasteurized at these times and food should not be cooked at temperatures less than 131°F / 55°C for more than 4 hours.

While there are slight differences in the heating time for different temperatures of water baths, the times usually vary less than 5 to 10% even going from a 111°F / 44°C bath to a 141°F / 60.5°C bath, which equates to a difference of 5 minutes every hour. We show the largest value in our chart, so if you are cooking it at a lower temperature you can knock a little of the time off.

Pasteurize from Refrigerator to 131°F / 55°C

This is the amount of time it will take a piece of meat that is 41°F / 5°C to become pasteurized in a 131°F / 55°C water bath.

Pasteurize from Refrigerator to 141°F / 60.5°C

This is the amount of time it will take a piece of meat that is 41°F / 5°C to become pasteurized in a 141°F / 60.5°C water bath.

Heat from Refrigerator to Any Temperature

70mm	6h 25m
65mm	5h 30m
60mm	4h 45m
55mm	4h 0m 0s
50mm	3h 15m
45mm	2h 40m
40mm	2h 10m
35mm	1h 40m
30mm	1h 15m 0s
25mm	0h 50m
20mm	0h 35m
15mm	0h 20m
10mm	0h 8m
5mm	0h 2m 0s

Heat from Freezer to Any Temperature

70mm	7 hrs 40 mins
65mm	6 hrs 40 mins
60mm	5 hrs 35 mins
55mm	4 hrs 45 mins
50mm	4 hrs 00 mins
45mm	3 hrs 10 mins
40mm	2 hrs 30 mins
35mm	2 hrs 00 mins
30mm	1 hrs 30 mins
25mm	1 hrs 00 mins
20mm	0 hrs 40 mins
15mm	0 hrs 25 mins
10mm	0 hrs 10 mins
5mm	0 hrs 02 mins

Pasteurize from Refrigerator to 131°F / 55°C

70mm	5 hrs 15 mins
65mm	4 hrs 45 mins
60mm	4 hrs 15 mins
55mm	3 hrs 50 mins
50mm	3 hrs 25 mins
45mm	3 hrs 00 mins
40mm	2 hrs 40 mins
35mm	2 hrs 20 mins
30mm	2 hrs 00 mins
25mm	1 hrs 50 mins
20mm	1 hrs 40 mins
15mm	1 hrs 30 mins
10mm	1 hrs 25 mins
5mm	1 hrs 20 mins

Pasteurize from Refrigerator to 141°F / 60.5°C

70mm	3 hrs 50 mins
65mm	3 hrs 25 mins
60mm	3 hrs 00 mins
55mm	2 hrs 40 mins
50mm	2 hrs 20 mins
45mm	2 hrs 00 mins
40mm	1 hrs 40 mins
35mm	1 hrs 25 mins
30mm	1 hrs 10 mins
25mm	0 hrs 55 mins
20mm	0 hrs 45 mins
15mm	0 hrs 35 mins
10mm	0 hrs 25 mins
5mm	0 hrs 21 mins

CHICKEN THICKNESS CHART

Pasteurize from Refrigerator to 135.5°F / 57.5°C

This is the amount of time it will take a piece of chicken that is 41°F / 5°C to become pasteurized in a 135.5°F / 57.5°C water bath.

Pasteurize from Refrigerator to 141°F / 60.5°C

This is the amount of time it will take a piece of chicken that is 41°F / 5°C to become pasteurized in a 141°F / 60.5°C water bath.

Pasteurize from Refrigerator to 146.3°F / 63.5°C

This is the amount of time it will take a piece of chicken that is 41°F / 5°C to become pasteurized in a 146.3°F / 63.5°C water bath.

Pasteurize from Refrigerator to 150.8°F / 66°C

This is the amount of time it will take a piece of chicken that is 41°F / 5°C to become pasteurized in a 150.8°F / 66°C water bath.

Pasteurize from Refrigerator to 135.5°F / 57.5°C

70mm	6h 30m
65mm	6h
60mm	5h 15m
55mm	4h 45m
50mm	4h 15m
45mm	3h 45m
40mm	3h 20m
35mm	3h
30mm	2h 35m
25mm	2h 20m
20mm	2h 5m
15mm	1h 55m
10mm	1h 45m
5mm	1h 40m

Pasteurize from Refrigerator to 141°F / 60.5°C

70mm	4h 55m
65mm	4h 20m
60mm	3h 50m
55mm	3h 20m
50mm	2h 55m
45mm	2h 30m
40mm	2h 5m
35mm	1h 45m
30mm	1h 25m
25mm	1h 10m
20mm	0h 55m
15mm	0h 45m
10mm	0h 36m
5mm	0h 31m

Pasteurize from Refrigerator to 146.3°F / 63.5°C

70mm	4h 0m 0s
65mm	3h 35m
60mm	3h 10m
55mm	2h 45m
50mm	2h 20m
45mm	2h
40mm	1h 40m
35mm	1h 20m
30mm	1h
25mm	0h 50m
20mm	0h 35m
15mm	0h 23m
10mm	0h 15m
5mm	0h 10m

Pasteurize from Refrigerator to 150.8°F / 66°C

70mm	3h 35m 0s
65mm	3h 10m
60mm	2h 45m
55mm	2h 20m
50mm	2h
45mm	1h 40m
40mm	1h 25m
35mm	1h 5m
30mm	0h 50m
25mm	0h 40m
20mm	0h 26m
15mm	0h 20m
10mm	0h 10m
5mm	0h 5m

Heat Fatty Fish to Any Temperature

These times show how long it will take to heat an entire piece of fatty fish from 41°F / 5°C to any typical temperature.

Reminder, this food might not be pasteurized at these times and food should not be cooked at temperatures less than 131°F / 55°C for more than 4 hours.

While there are slight differences in the heating time for different temperatures of water baths, the times usually vary less than 5 to 10% even going from a 111°F / 44°C bath to a 141°F / 60.5°C bath, which equates to a difference of 5 minutes every hour. We show the largest value in our chart, so if you are cooking it at a lower temperature you can knock a little of the time off.

Pasteurize Lean Fish to 131°F / 55°C

This is the amount of time it will take a piece of lean fish that is 41°F / 5°C to become pasteurized in a 131°F / 55°C water bath.

Pasteurize Lean Fish to 141°F / 60.5°C

This is the amount of time it will take a piece of lean fish that is 41°F / 5°C to become pasteurized in a 141°F / 60.5°C water bath.

Pasteurize Fatty Fish to 131°F / 55°C

This is the amount of time it will take a piece of fatty fish that is 41°F / 5°C to become pasteurized in a 131°F / 55°C water bath.

Pasteurize Fatty Fish to 141°F / 60.5°C

This is the amount of time it will take a piece of fatty fish that is 41°F / 5°C to become pasteurized in a 141°F / 60.5°C water bath.

Heat Fatty Fish to Any Temperature

70mm	6 hrs 25 mins
65mm	5 hrs 30 mins
60mm	4 hrs 45 mins
55mm	4 hrs 00 mins
50mm	3 hrs 15 mins
45mm	2 hrs 40 mins
40mm	2 hrs 10 mins
35mm	1 hrs 40 mins
30mm	1 hrs 15 mins
25mm	0 hrs 50 mins
20mm	0 hrs 35 mins
15mm	0 hrs 20 mins
10mm	0 hrs 08 mins
5mm	0 hrs 02 mins

Pasteurize Lean Fish to 131°F / 55°C

70mm	5 hrs 15 mins
65mm	4 hrs 45 mins
60mm	4 hrs 15 mins
55mm	3 hrs 50 mins
50mm	3 hrs 25 mins
45mm	3 hrs 00 mins
40mm	2 hrs 40 mins
35mm	2 hrs 20 mins
30mm	2 hrs 00 mins
25mm	1 hrs 50 mins
20mm	1 hrs 40 mins
15mm	1 hrs 30 mins
10mm	1 hrs 25 mins
5mm	1 hrs 20 mins

Pasteurize Lean Fish to 141°F / 60.5°C

70mm	6 hrs 30 mins
65mm	6 hrs 00 mins
60mm	5 hrs 15 mins
55mm	4 hrs 45 mins
50mm	4 hrs 15 mins
45mm	3 hrs 45 mins
40mm	3 hrs 20 mins
35mm	3 hrs 00 mins
30mm	2 hrs 35 mins
25mm	2 hrs 20 mins
20mm	2 hrs 05 mins
15mm	1 hrs 55 mins
10mm	1 hrs 45 mins
5mm	1 hrs 40 mins

Pasteurize Fatty Fish to 131°F / 55°C

70mm	5 hrs 15 mins
65mm	4 hrs 45 mins
60mm	4 hrs 15 mins
55mm	3 hrs 50 mins
50mm	3 hrs 25 mins
45mm	3 hrs 00 mins
40mm	2 hrs 40 mins
35mm	2 hrs 20 mins
30mm	2 hrs 00 mins
25mm	1 hrs 50 mins
20mm	1 hrs 40 mins
15mm	1 hrs 30 mins
10mm	1 hrs 25 mins
5mm	1 hrs 20 mins

Pasteurize Fatty Fish to 141°F / 60.5°C

70mm	6 hrs 30 mins
65mm	6 hrs 00 mins
60mm	5 hrs 15 mins
55mm	4 hrs 45 mins
50mm	4 hrs 15 mins
45mm	3 hrs 45 mins
40mm	3 hrs 20 mins
35mm	3 hrs 00 mins
30mm	2 hrs 35 mins
25mm	2 hrs 20 mins
20mm	2 hrs 05 mins
15mm	1 hrs 55 mins
10mm	1 hrs 45 mins
5mm	1 hrs 40 mins

SOUS VIDE RESOURCES

For an up to date look at current books, websites, and other sous vide resources you can visit the list we keep on our website.

You can find it at:
www.cookingsousvide.com/info/sous-vide-resources

Sous vide is a very complex process and there is much more to learn about it besides what has been covered in this book. There is more and more good information available about sous vide cooking. Here are some resources to help you continue to learn more.

BOOKS

Under Pressure
By Thomas Keller

This book shows you the extent of what is possible through sous vide cooking. The recipes aren't easy, and they require a lot of work but they can provide great inspiration for dishes of your own. If you are interested in expanding your concept of what can be accomplished through cooking then this is a must have.

Cooking for Geeks
By Jeff Potter

If you are interested in the Geekier aspects of cooking then this book does a great job. It takes you through the basics of setting up your kitchen all the way up to kitchen hacks and sous vide cooking.

On Food and Cooking
By Harold McGee

This is the ultimate guide to the scientific aspects of cooking. If you like to know why things happen in the kitchen, at every level, you'll find this book fascinating.

Beginning Sous Vide: Low Temperature Recipes and Techniques for Getting Started at Home
By Jason Logsdon

Our main book covering sous vide. It deals a lot with the various equipment options and has over 100 recipes, some of which have been specially adapted for this book. It is available from Amazon.com or on our website.

Sous Vide Grilling
By Jason Logsdon

Our book that is focused on grilling and BBQ recipes. It includes 95 great recipes covering steaks, burgers, kebabs, pulled pork, and everything in between. It is available from Amazon.com or on our website.

Cooking Sous Vide: A Guide for the Home Cook
By Jason Logsdon

My first book and the first book written exclusively for the home cook learning sous vide. Most of the information from it has been updated and adapted for inclusion in Beginning Sous Vide.

Sous-Vide Cuisine

By Joan Roca

From the authors: "we propose our book, as a progression that involves three concepts of sous-vide: Storage, Cooking and Cuisine." Be sure to get a copy that is in English, as many copies are not.

Modernist Cuisine: The Art and Science of Cooking

By Nathan Myhrvold

This just released and aims to be the bible of modernist cuisine. It's over 2,400 pages costs $500 and was several years in the making. If you are serious about learning the newly developing modernist techniques then this might be worth the investment.

Sous Vide for the Home Cook

By Douglas Baldwin

Baldwin helped to define and codify home sous vide cooking with his free online guide. His book is a nice intro to the subject, including food safety, and has many simple recipes to follow.

Sous Vide

By Viktor Stampfer

A collection of some of Viktor's best sous vide recipes. Be sure to get a copy that is in English, as many copies are not.

WEBSITES

Cooking Sous Vide

http://www.cookingsousvide.com

This is the main website where I contribute sous vide articles. We update it regularly with original recipes and news from around the sous vide community. There are also community features such as forums and question and answer pages.

SVKitchen

http://www.svkitchen.com

A great site on sous vide cooking and one I read constantly. They touch on everything from standard sous vide swordfish to making your own preserved lemons with sous vide.

Sous Vide: Recipes, Techniques & Equipment

http://forums.egullet.org/index.php?showtopic=116617&st=0

A very long forum string from eGullet, about 98 pages long at this time that covers almost everything you need to know about sous vide if you have the time to look through it all. I suggest starting near the end and working towards the front.

APPS

We also have two apps for the iPhone and iPad available, as well as one for the Android. You can search in the app store for "Sous Vide" and ours should be near the top, published by "Primolicious".

PAPERS AND RESEARCH

USDA Guide

http://www.fsis.usda.gov/OPPDE/rdad/FSISNotices/RTE_Poultry_Tables.pdf

The US government guide to poultry and beef cooking times.

Practical Guide to Sous Vide

http://amath.colorado.edu/~baldwind/sous-vide.html

Written by Douglas Baldwin, this is one of the best guides available for the scientific principles behind sous vide cooking and a pioneering work in home sous vide cooking.

Sous Vide Safety

http://www.seriouseats.com/2010/04/sous-vide-basics-low-temperature-chicken.html

A nice look at the basics of low temperature cooking, specifically as it applies to chicken.

RECIPE INDEX

CPSIA information can be obtained at www.ICGtesting.com
Printed in the USA
BVOW080018240112

281224BV00005B/18/P

9 781466 381285